The God We Worship

Robert: May God's grace fill your life with love.
Sondra Matthaei
7/16/98

The God We Worship

Sondra Higgins Matthaei

CHARLES W. BROCKWELL, JR.
GENERAL EDITOR

Abingdon Press / Nashville

THE GOD WE WORSHIP

This book is printed on acid-free, recycled paper.

Library of Congress Cataloging-in-Publication Data

Matthaei, Sondra Higgins,
The God we worship / Sondra Higgins Matthaei.
p. cm.
Includes bibliographical references and index.
ISBN 0-687-15203-8
1. God. 2. United Methodist Church (U.S.)—Doctrines. 3. Methodist Church—Doctrines. I. Title.
BT102.M357 1993
231—dc20 93-8154
CIP

Those noted KJV are from the King James or Authorized Version of the Bible.

93 94 95 96 97 98 99 00 01 02—10 9 8 7 6 5 4 3 2 1

MANUFACTURED IN THE UNITED STATES OF AMERICA

TO MY PARENTS,

Paul and Marj Matthaei

Contents

Foreword

This is a book I wish had been available when I began my ministry more than forty years ago. Teaching was always a large component of my pastoral ministry. When I first read this book, I "itched" for the opportunity to use it with a group of persons who wanted to explore their faith in depth.

Having said that, I hasten to add that it is not a leader's guide or a teacher's manual. It is a tool which may be used with equal value for individual reflection or as a group study and reflection guide. It respects the adult believer in the way it presents its material. It challenges persons to grow as they reflect on their faith, share it with others, receive the experiences of others, and continue the process of reflection and faith formation.

The subject of the book, the God we worship, is the basic foundation of our faith. Theology is the study of God. These facts alone suggest that this book should be of great interest to move theology into the life of its users and out of the province of professional theologians.

The four principal sources for United Methodist theological reflection are Scripture, tradition, experience, and reason. Those who take this book seriously will discover that it calls for interactive use and reflection on all these sources as the reader seeks to understand the God we worship. It is really a manual in "doing theology" using the basic resources that are important to the followers of John Wesley.

This book is timely because it helps to relate theology to life. There is a common assumption in our culture that theology is an idle pursuit. Our values are determined by television and our behavior is shaped by peer-group pressure. Laypersons need all the resources they can find to assist in transforming the Bible from a revered relic full of noble thoughts to a source of insight for everyday living.

As a glance at the appendixes will reveal, the book is deeply grounded in basic documents of the church. The appendixes themselves are helpful references.

I believe God will bless this book to help laypersons understand their heritage, plan for the present, and shape their future.

R. Sheldon Duecker

Preface

Bishop R. Sheldon Duecker has asserted, "United Methodists don't have a *common* understanding of basic Christian beliefs." He has reported a layperson saying to him, "I hunger for a clear sense of my United Methodist *identity*."

What is United Methodist doctrine? Many voices respond to this question, ranging from those hoping to instruct the church to caucuses intending to pressure it.

None of these voices, however, speaks for the church. "No person, no paper, no organization, has the authority to speak officially for The United Methodist Church, this right having been reserved exclusively to the General Conference under the Constitution" (*The Book of Discipline,* par. 610.1).

This book is the third of a series called "We Believe." This is a series of books written for United Methodist laypersons to advance self-understanding and identity by communicating United Methodist doctrine directly from General Conference approved documents.

The authors have set forth what the church officially teaches rather than what each thinks the church ought to teach. They focus on the question: "What theological teaching has The United Methodist Church 'owned' through its established conciliar processes of decision making and teaching?"

Thus these books are not personal statements or caucus declarations.

They present the teachings of John Wesley, *The Book of Discipline,* and other official United Methodist documents (e.g., *The Book of Resolutions, The United Methodist Hymnal, The Book of Services*).

The authors in this series do not proceed by linking up the categories of systematic theology and saying what the church teaches under each heading. They pursue core elements of "substantial, experimental, practical divinity" through the church's own documents. This method of beginning with how doctrine affects Christian life is characteristically Wesleyan.

John Wesley used our doctrines to specify the scriptural, historic Christian teachings that were the particular emphases of "the work of God called Methodism." Primarily, these were teachings relating to divine-human interaction and to sanctification. The books in this series remind us of this heritage and include United Methodist, not just Wesleyan, doctrine.

What might these books do for The United Methodist Church? (1) They will bring before the church its common body of official doctrinal sources and survey what these sources teach. (2) They will demonstrate how the church's workbooks and worship books are doctrinal documents. (3) They will advance the teaching office of the General Conference. (4) They will point out where the church's doctrine needs clarification and better organization for consistency and coherence. (5) They will promote discussion of whether the church needs a theological secretariat to assist our highest governing council in defining United Methodist doctrine.

The United Methodist Church is part of the community of Wesleyan denominations, but The United Methodist Church has larger responsibilities. One of these is the formal development of doctrine. The books in this series contribute to the maturing of that ministry among and for "the people called United Methodists."

Charles W. Brockwell, Jr.
General Editor

Introduction

LIFE IS A JOURNEY IN RELATIONSHIP, WITH OTHER PERSONS AND WITH GOD. This book is about the journey of faith and the ways people come to know God. The task of this book is to help United Methodists grow in their relationship with God through theological reflection on the doctrine of God.

Because theological reflection is both an individual and a group task, this book is designed for either individual or group use. Throughout the book guidance on topics for reflection is given in *italic* print. Persons who choose to use the book individually may ignore the *italic* instructions or use them for personal reflection.

The Study Session Guide (pp. 99-106) offers additional options for group study. Study sessions for a class may be planned around each chapter, or chapters 2 through 4 may be divided into three study sessions each for more in-depth work. In order to create an environment for thoughtful reflection, it is important for group members to listen carefully to one another as they discuss their faith. Because faith is a deeply personal matter, participants should recognize the courage it takes for others to share.

The God We Worship is part of the We Believe series, which addresses important aspects of faith through study of doctrinal themes as understood in The United Methodist Church. The first volume published in the series, *The Gospel of Grace* by Kenneth Kinghorn, explores our understanding of grace in the Wesleyan tradition through study of John Wesley's *via salutis,* the way of salvation. A second book, *God Made Known* by Thomas Langford, is an important examination of the relationship between doctrine and theological reflection. It introduces us to the doctrinal standards of The United Methodist Church and the use of Scripture, tradition, experience, and reason as the sources and criteria for theological reflection.

The God We Worship is integrally related to the two books that have preceded it because reflection about the nature of God and God's activity in the world cannot be done in isolation. Our understanding of God cannot be isolated from discussions of human sinfulness or God's redeeming act in Jesus Christ. Our doctrinal standards are accountable to the record of God's action in history as recorded in the Bible and interpreted through Christian tradition. Though recognizing the interrelationships of the total faith enterprise, the focus of this book is on God, our Creator and the author of salvation.

The General Conference of The United Methodist Church has provided us with the primary resource documents for this study: *The Book of Discipline (BOD), The Book of Resolutions (BOR), The Book of Worship (BOW), The United Methodist Hymnal (UMH),* and *The COCU Consensus (COCUC).* The intent is for you to work with these resources throughout your study. Some quotations from our United Methodist documents are included in the text for your use in case you do not have the primary resource documents readily available.

Other important sources come from the growing library of Wesleyan scholarship, including *The Works of John Wesley, The Limits of Love Divine, Aldersgate Reconsidered, Mirror and Memory, John Wesley's Experimental Divinity,* and *What United Methodists Should Teach.* Additional resources come from a connectional system which provides us with numerous study resources to contribute to our growth in faith: *Doctrinal Standards and Our Theological Task, This We Believe, Words That Hurt, Words That Heal,* and *Language of Hospitality.*

Resources used in this work include articles and books listed in the annotated bibliography with their abbreviations, which appear in the text and the endnotes. Quotations from the primary texts are altered in places for a more inclusive reading. Substituted words are enclosed in brackets. Scripture references from the *New Revised Standard Version* are included in each chapter, but selected additional references can be found in appendix 3. Further biblical references can be found in any concordance under the heading given in the appendix.

Finally, I want to thank those persons who have contributed to this project through their support and input. Dr. Warren Carter was a substantive dialogue partner in developing the interpretation of the biblical texts and in clarifying the project as a whole. I am deeply appreciative of my editor, Charles Brockwell, whose vision and gracious guidance helped give birth to a dialogical style of writing. And, as United Methodists, we owe a debt of gratitude to Abingdon Press for creating this series to help us learn more about our heritage of faith.

Sondra Matthaei
1993

The God We Worship

CHAPTER ONE

Preparation for the Journey

FAITH IN GOD INVOLVES A LIFELONG PROCESS OF GROWTH THROUGH OUR RELATIONSHIPS WITH OTHER PERSONS AND WITH GOD. This book is about our faith in God. It addresses questions about who God is and what God has done, what we believe as individuals and what we believe as a church. We will be exploring the documents of The United Methodist Church to determine if the church's understanding of God has changed over time.

Before you read further, stop and take time to remember the story of your relationship with God. In what ways has your relationship with God developed?

As a young child, my image of God was that of *Creator*, a kind, grandfatherly man who lived "out there" somewhere. This God created the world in which we live and was much like significant adults in my life who wanted me to be good and who would punish me if I was really bad. But even from this early age, I knew that God was someone who always loved me, no matter what I did.

In my elementary and adolescent years, I learned about a God who took human form and lived on earth. The human Jesus showed us how God wanted us to live—taking care of the sick, feeding the hungry, giving drink to the thirsty, and clothing the naked. But even more than that, Jesus was willing to die as a witness to God's great love for us. Jesus became Christ, our Savior and *Redeemer*. Yet as a teenager, I remember thinking repeatedly, "Why do we use words like incarnation, atonement, justification, assurance, and salvation—words that don't make sense anymore? Why don't we talk about God in language people can understand?"

As an adult, my relationship with God is much more complex. It has been shaped by life experiences in which I have known God as *Sustainer,* the comforting presence in my life. But my knowledge about God and my experience of God have also been informed by studying Scripture and church tradition through participation in the faith community.

My story undoubtedly reflects an experience common to many of us. As we grow older, we learn more from our life experience, and this knowledge brings us new insights into our faith. And as we learn more about our faith, we gain new perspective on the meaning of our lives. But with new insights come new questions.

Take a few moments to think about and share the ways your understanding of God has changed or grown across your lifetime. What are your images for God? What questions do you have about God?

Our Theological Task

By telling our faith stories, we have begun to think theologically, to reflect on how God has acted in our lives. Our task in this study is to grow in our understanding of God through theological exploration of what we believe, our doctrine of God.

In *God Made Known,* Tom Langford tells us that "doctrine is the declaration of the collective understanding of the Church expressed in agreed-upon formulations such as creeds" (*GMKL,* 40). He also teaches us that the church's doctrine and theological exploration go hand-in-hand because theological reflection is "doctrine in the making . . . doctrine stretched in new directions" (*GMKL,* 40).

In this book, we will examine the images of God and language about God found in documents "owned" by the General Conference of The United Methodist Church. In addition to Bibles and Bible commentaries, you or your group will need at least one copy of the latest versions of *The Book of Discipline (BOD)*, *The Book of Resolutions (BOR)*, *The Book of Worship (BOW)*, and *The United Methodist Hymnal (UMH)* for reference (check with your pastor, church library, or conference office for copies). The General Conference of our church has given us these documents for our study and growth, to inspire us to live as Christ's faithful disciples. In our exploration, we will be studying the most recent versions of these resources.

This call to continuing reflection in The United Methodist Church is a tradition shared with the larger Christian community. As we join biblical writers in attempting to find ways to name how God has been at work in our lives, we discover this tradition is both a gift and a challenge. It is a gift to be free to think about matters of faith, knowing that God is with us in that task. But it is a challenge also, because sometimes we would prefer that our church tell us straight and simple what to believe.

At those times of uncertainty, growth, or transition on our faith journeys, we need to hear the Christian story again and again. We can rely on the account of what God has done as revealed in Scripture, on the witness of faith from all the saints who have preceded us, and on the collective wisdom of our own faith community to guide our lives. But with every new generation, life experiences require us to name once again what God has done for us. The New Testament writers make frequent reference to passages from the Hebrew Bible as they reinterpret God's action from the past for the present.[1] So, too, we must reinterpret God's work in the world for our time.

Take a few moments to examine the ways in which the New Testament writers reinterpret the Hebrew Bible for their time by reading the following pairs of scripture: Hosea 11:1 and Matthew 2:15; Psalm 22:1 and Matthew 27:46. What happens in each reinterpretation? Is there a change of symbol, of language, of meaning? Be sure to note any changes in images or names for God.

Sometimes the "old" language or symbols do not work for us, so we have to create new ways to share the Good News with one another. Sometimes our life experiences challenge our faith and what we thought we believed. The gifts from the past and the experiences of the present cause us to reflect once more on what God has done for us. Ultimately, our reflection calls us to respond to God's action in faith, to live as Christian disciples.

Sources and Criteria for the Process of Reflection

We are introduced to the Wesleyan quadrilateral of Scripture, tradition, experience, and reason in *God Made Known* (*GMKL,* 73ff.). These four sources and criteria for theological reflection help us think together about who God is and what God has done (*BOD,* par. 68, pp. 76-82). As we study together, we can trust that God will work through our theological exploration to bring us new insights as we seek to grow in faith.

The way we use the quadrilateral is called our theological method, or the process we use to think about God. We do this in different ways. Sometimes we start by reading or recalling *Scripture*. We may study what scholars have taught us about a particular book or passage, or we may read the Scripture meditatively. As we approach the Scripture, however, we eventually ask the question, What does it mean for us? And that leads us to consider our own faith *experience*. When we ask, What has this passage meant for persons of faith across the centuries? we move into an examination of *tradition*. Throughout this process of exploration, we use *reason* to guide our thinking.

A different theological approach may start with *experience*. If we have a life crisis that calls into question all that we believe, we may turn to *Scripture* to help us find strength and meaning. Or we might find a biography of a person of faith from our *tradition*—the story of one who struggled with life's challenges and found a way through those challenges in faith. Through *reason*, we use the Wesleyan quadrilateral to find meaning in our times of challenge.

We may start our reflection with any part of the Wesleyan quadrilateral, but *our theological exploration is not complete until we engage all four sources and criteria: Scripture, tradition, experience, and reason.* Our reflection finally will be accountable to the authoritative revelation of God's action recorded in Scripture.

Take some time to think about your way of reflecting. You might want to write down some ideas or symbolize how you would work with the Wesleyan quadrilateral. Do you think your own theological method will start most often with Scripture? with tradition? with experience? with reason? What are some examples of how you might think theologically?

It is to be expected that those of us who study together will do our theological exploration in a variety of ways. As we share with one another, new insights will come through hearing ideas from our different points of view. The result of sharing our unique perspectives is that we learn more about the variety of ways God has acted in our lives and gain insight into how we might continue to respond in faith.

But how do we know that our thoughts and actions reflect God's truth and not our human desires? Theological reflection requires collective discernment. *Discernment* means to recognize or see God's truth more clearly so that we might be more faithful. *Collective discernment* is a task we do together. The gift of discernment is cultivated by sharing Scripture, study, prayer, and decision making with others in our church. Sharing understandings of our faith response in light of what God has done helps us be more accountable to God's truth in our daily lives. We provide "checks and balances" for one another.

The process of collective discernment is part of our faith tradition. Following in the footsteps of Brother Lawrence who lived in the seventeenth century, Dwayne Huebner of Princeton University calls this collective discernment "practicing the presence of God":

> To be religious is to be with God in the world with others. . . . It may be an awareness of God's grace, discipline, redemption, or gifts; a commitment to God's ways, laws, and love; a celebration of God's covenants and mighty deeds; or merely a sense of God's presence and our faithful response. Practicing that presence requires more or less constant awareness of or reference to God in our life.[2]

The question for us is *how* we will maintain a "constant reference to God" in our lives.

The Quaker practice of a "Clearness Committee" may give us some help in discerning God's truth together. A clearness committee is rooted in the conviction that God is present to help us with our life decisions. According to Parker Palmer, "The clearness committee can help people discover their own God-given leadings and callings through silence, through questioning, through listening, through prayer." The clearness committee begins with "a period of centering silence" followed by one person sharing her or his question. The focus of the group is on helping that person find God's direction. Members of the committee ask "honest, caring questions," and the person responds as the questions are asked. But the person always has the right not to answer. The committee reflects in silence and prayer as a way to hear God's truth in their midst.[3]

We will be called to use the gift of discernment as we explore what we believe about God. Take some time to think about how you will practice the presence of God "through silence, through questioning, through listening, through prayer." When will you need to use each of these means of discernment? How will you know which is needed?

Wrestling Jacob

We will be using Charles Wesley's great hymn "Come, O Thou Traveler Unknown" to frame our study of the God we worship (*UMH* #386). Charles often wrote hymns to express the heart of John Wesley's theological thought. This hymn is based on a poem called "Wrestling Jacob" (*UMH* #387). Two striking metaphors from this hymn symbolize our work together.

The first is the metaphor of journey. Our lives are journeys of faith. Like the people whose stories we find in Scripture, we may face rocky paths, dangerous stretches of highway, or desert places. Sometimes the road is winding, and we cannot see our way ahead. At times, our road is blocked, and we take detours; but we travel on our journeys in faith. As we proceed on our spiritual journeys, we seek to understand our experiences through the eyes of faith. Reflecting theologically on our spiritual journeys is consistent with our Wesleyan heritage. Historian Richard P.

Heitzenrater notes, "For [Wesley], theological reflection is inexorably tied to the spiritual pilgrimage, and both are dynamic and developmental" (*MMH,* 148). Spiritual pilgrimage and theological reflection are partners for spiritual growth.

The second metaphor from Wesley's hymn is that of wrestling. Theological exploration is not an easy task. Sometimes we feel as if we are wrestling with ourselves and never will be clear about our faith. Sometimes we disagree with one another and exhaust ourselves in the struggle. Sometimes we seem to wrestle with God. We are not alone in our wrestling. Many of the Psalms, as well as Jesus' prayer in Gethsemane, are examples of biblical expressions of this struggle to understand God's ways.

Journey and *wrestling* are appropriate action metaphors for our theological reflection within The United Methodist Church. Today the Methodist "family" continues to wrestle with what it means to be united in the midst of diversity. M. Douglas Meeks from Wesley Seminary describes the discussions of our shared heritage by Methodist scholars who gathered at Oxford in 1987:

> We have spoken fairly often about being a Methodist "family." But the family members do not want a quick consensus and an easy unity. Who will define the consensus? We have heard several different responses to that question. . . . And so our debate has moved: sometimes at a snail's pace, quite often with consternation, occasionally with anger, but, in it all, as a family discussion around the *only* table which in these times is likely to keep the family together at all. (*WSMT,* 132)

Even in the midst of diversity and wrestling, United Methodists find unity with one another at the Communion Table.

Mary Elizabeth Moore from the School of Theology at Claremont, California, has used the journey metaphor to characterize how United Methodists do theology in another way: "United Methodists do theology—on the run!"[4] Time does not stand still and wait for decisions to be made. As the church, we make decisions about our living witness through our understanding of the Christian story and what God is calling us to do. Together we reflect theologically on our actions in order to reinterpret God's call to discipleship in our own lives and to make new decisions about our actions. It is a never-ending cycle of dreaming or visioning, deciding, acting, reevaluating, and dreaming again. And throughout the journey, we wrestle with life's challenges as we try to be faithful to God's truth.

A Look Ahead

We began this journey of faith at our birth, first trusting the significant adults around us to give us love and care. As we grew, we tried at different times and in different ways to make sense of our lives through the eyes of faith. In this book, we are continuing our journey by reflecting on our relationship with God, by reviewing our understanding of doctrine and theological exploration, and by learning about theological method and the process of discernment.

Let us open our minds and hearts to one another and to God as we spend some time together thinking about God—the One beyond us *(Creator),* the One among us *(Redeemer),* and the One within us *(Sustainer)*—as we ask, Who is the God we worship?

Make a list of the names or images that you use for God. Then add the names for God you find in this chapter.

In the next chapter we will explore the images of God in the biblical witness and join Charles Wesley in imploring God to journey with us:

> Come, O thou Traveler unknown,
> whom still I hold, but cannot see!
> My company before is gone,
> and I am left alone with thee;
> with thee all night I mean to stay
> and wrestle till the break of day.
> (*UMH* #387)

Chapter 3 will help us look at our inherited witness to the nature of God as Trinity in the creeds, in the foundational documents of The United Methodist Church, and in a document from our ecumenical dialogues. In chapter 4, we will use a study of the gospel feast and Wesley's understanding of the *via salutis* (the way of salvation) to reflect on our understanding of God as the One who creates us and invites us to reconciliation, the One who redeems us and provides a way of salvation, and the One who sustains us and is with us as we respond in faith. In the final chapter, we will have an opportunity to conclude our study and to celebrate our God of many names through our inherited witness in hymns and prayers. Issues of cultural and gender diversity in understanding God, as well as the language of faith in talking about God, will be explored.

As we continue, let us remember that our journey holds a promise, the promise that God is with us and will bless us as we wrestle with our doubts on the path to faith. In those moments of blessing, our differences about belief, images, or language will be celebrated as we share Charles Wesley's great affirmation of faith:

> 'Tis Love! 'tis Love! thou diedst for me,
> I hear thy whisper in my heart.
> The morning breaks, the shadows flee,
> pure Universal Love thou art:
> to me, to all, thy mercies move—
> thy nature, and thy name is Love.
> (*UMH* #387)

CHAPTER TWO

Come, O Thou Traveler Unknown

The Biblical Witness

THE BIBLE BEARS WITNESS TO A VARIETY OF IMAGES AND NAMES FOR GOD. Our exploration of the biblical witness will begin with the story of Jacob's remarkable relationship with God. In the second part of this chapter, we will turn to one of John Wesley's most famous sermons, "Salvation by Faith," based on Ephesians 2:8, to examine Wesley's understanding of the greatest blessing God has given us. And finally, we will reflect together on how God's blessing becomes our invitation to discipleship in a study of the Beatitudes.

Throughout this chapter, the emphasis is on God's relationship with a community, God's covenant with a people. The faith experiences of the persons we will study were shaped by their participation in a community. In turn, their responses to God's call affected the continuing life of their communities. The heart of the biblical message is that God chooses to be in relationship with us as a people.

In each part of our study, we will be asking two questions of Scripture: Who is God and what has God done? We will try to answer these questions through the eyes of Jacob, the sermon of John Wesley, and Jesus' teachings in the Sermon on the Mount. We will be using all four sources and criteria from the Wesleyan quadrilateral in our study of the biblical witness to the nature of God.

One word at the heart of this chapter is *blessing*. For us, a blessing usually indicates approval or favor. But in the biblical tradition, a blessing is a life-changing event. A blessing is a statement that changes the life of the hearer. In his book *Genesis,* Walter Brueggemann describes a blessing as the power of the spoken word to shape human lives. A blessing from God is a bestowal of divine favor initiating a special vocation.[1] The recipient of a blessing is a person or community called by God. But a biblical blessing is never private. It shapes the vocation of a people. Once a blessing is given, it is passed on to future generations and thus binds families or communities together across the centuries.

A Tale of Deceit and Blessing

The story of Jacob reads like a modern-day screenplay. It is a tale of deception and intrigue. Genesis 27:1-45 tells how Jacob and his mother deceive Isaac, Jacob's dying father. The deception results in Isaac giving Jacob the blessing that rightfully belongs to the older brother, Esau. Isaac blesses Jacob, who is disguised as Esau, saying,

> May God give you of the dew of heaven,
> and of the fatness of the earth,
> and plenty of grain and wine.
> Let peoples serve you,
> and nations bow down to you.
> Be lord over your brothers,
> and may your mother's sons bow down to you.
> Cursed be everyone who curses you,
> and blessed be everyone who blesses you!
> (Gen. 27:28-29)

Once the deception is discovered, it is too late. The blessing has already been given, and Esau vows revenge.

Take some time to read the story of Jacob's deception in Genesis 27:1-45. How would you feel if you were Isaac, Jacob, Rebekah, Esau? How does the blessing change Jacob's life? What questions does this account raise for you?

Consequences come with every blessing. The result of Isaac's blessing on Jacob is that Jacob has to run away to escape his brother's wrath. Jacob becomes a fugitive. The blessing Jacob wanted so much becomes a burden and forces him to begin a long journey in exile.

Jacob's story continues in Genesis 28:10-22 when he and his company stop for the night to rest. As Jacob sleeps, he dreams of a ladder to heaven with God's messengers ascending and descending. In this dream, God stands beside Jacob and says,

> I am the LORD, the God of Abraham your father and the God of Isaac; the land on which you lie I will give to you and to your offspring; and your offspring shall be like the dust of the earth, and you shall spread abroad to the west and to the east and to the north and to the south; and all the families of the earth shall be blessed in you and in your offspring. Know that I am with you and will keep you wherever you go, and will bring you back to this land; for I will not leave you until I have done what I have promised you. (vv. 13-15)

God comes to Jacob, the trickster, when he is most vulnerable in sleep and blesses him! Walter Brueggemann states that through the blessing, "this 'non-person' (i.e., exiled, threatened) is transformed by the coming of God to a person crucial for the promise."[2]

Read Genesis 28:10-22. What images of God are portrayed in this account? Reread what God says to Jacob. What does God promise Jacob? Why would God bless someone like Jacob? How does Jacob become a "person crucial for the promise"?

Jacob's response to this experience gives us some clues about his understanding of God. When Jacob awakes, he is afraid. He says, "Surely the LORD is in this place—and I did not know it!" (28:16). So Jacob creates a sanctuary in that place for this awesome God and names it Bethel. But Jacob also knows a God of promise. As Jacob remembers the dream, he repeats God's promise: "I am with you . . . [I] will keep you . . . [I] will bring you back to this land." In return, Jacob promises that of everything God gives him, he will give one tenth back to God (v. 22). Now Jacob has God's blessing and is bound to God just as he is bound to his father, Isaac.

Jacob continues on his journey, but in Genesis 31:13, God commands Jacob to return to Esau, to go home. The story continues in Genesis 32:1–33:17. Jacob is worried about meeting Esau. In a prayer, Jacob asks God to intercede on his behalf (32:9-12) and then makes elaborate plans to test Esau's frame of mind. He decides to send everyone, including his wives and children, ahead of himself. If Esau is still seeking revenge, he will kill those at the front of the company first, and Jacob will be able to save at least the last half of his company. Nightfall finds Jacob alone at the back of the camp. Although Jacob makes elaborate preparations for his expected meeting with Esau, he does not expect to meet a shadowy stranger and wrestle through the night.

Read Genesis 32:22-32 and develop your interpretation of the story. Who is the stranger? How can you use tradition, experience, and reason to help you understand this passage? Can you imagine yourself in Jacob's place? What do you think he thought and felt?

The meaning of this passage is not clear; several interpretations are possible. But one likely interpretation is that the stranger with no name is Yahweh. Walter Brueggemann believes that the narrator of this story purposely left the stranger a shadowy figure because the unknown is so much more powerful than the known. He writes: "It is part of the power of the wrestling that we do not know the name or see the face of the antagonist."[3]

Jacob and the stranger wrestle all night and, at daybreak, come to a draw. Jacob is physically stronger and still holds the stranger. He will not let go. In Genesis 32:26 Jacob tries to bargain with the stranger, offering release in exchange for a blessing. The stranger does not respond to this request. Charles Wesley's interpretative poem describes the offer:

> Yield to me now, for I am weak,
> but confident in self-despair!
> Speak to my heart, in blessing speak,
> be conquered by my instant prayer.
> Speak, or thou never hence shalt move,
> and tell me if thy name is Love.
> (*UMH* #386)

In Genesis 32:27-28, the stranger is the stronger one who gives Jacob a new name, a new identity, and new power as leader of God's people,

Israel. To know a person's name is to have power over him or her. To give a person a name is to assume an even greater power. In Genesis 32:29, Jacob asks an outrageous question and wants to know the stranger's name! Compare the Scripture account with Charles Wesley's interpretation as he attempts to capture the significance of this moment:

> I need not tell thee who I am,
> my misery and sin declare;
> thyself hast called me by my name,
> look on thy hands and read it there.
> But who, I ask thee, who art thou?
> Tell me thy name, and tell me now.
> (*UMH* #386)

The stranger does not respond and returns to Jacob's first request, blessing Jacob as day breaks.

If the stranger was Yahweh, it is something of a miracle that Jacob saw God face to face and wrestled God to a draw. Not only did Jacob survive the encounter, but also he was blessed by God in spite of his stubborn audacity. Once again, Charles Wesley speaks for Jacob:

> My prayer hath power with God; the grace
> unspeakable I now receive;
> through faith I see thee face to face,
> I see thee face to face, and live!
> In vain I have not wept and strove—
> thy nature, and thy name is Love.
> (*UMH* #387)

*Now read all the verses of Wesley's poem (*UMH *#387) that end with "till I thy name, thy nature know." Notice how the repeated demand to know God's name emphasizes the length and power of Jacob's struggle. Examine Genesis 32:22-32 for images and names for God. Who was God for Jacob? What did God do for Jacob? What are the consequences of blessing for Jacob and his people? Is the God we know both an awesome and a blessing God?*

Differing images of God are apparent in this story. There is the *gracious, forgiving God,* who comes to Jacob, the trickster, and promises, "I am with you, I will keep you, and I will bring you back to this land." God acts as promise-giver and promise-keeper and, in the end, brings Jacob home. Through the blessing, Jacob is bound to God and his people.

But God is also the *awesome, holy One,* who challenges Jacob throughout the night. This God does not use physical power to conquer Jacob but exercises the power of silence and the spoken word, giving Jacob a new name and new identity, Israel. This is the unnamed, naming God, the One who claims us, who gives us our identity and our vocation.

Jacob won the blessing of his father by deceit and the blessing of God through a struggle. These blessings brought him a new name and physical injury from the wrestling. Yet Jacob in his physical weakness would have more power in the future as the father of a nation than he had when he wrestled God to a draw with his physical strength. This idea of weakness in power and power in weakness points the reader of this story toward a significant theme of the New Testament.

It is important to note that Jacob's relationship with God is set within the larger social circumstances of a people. One way to read this account is to see Jacob as a symbol for the people—and for ourselves. When God made a covenant with Jacob, God was calling a people to a special vocation. From that time on, the people of Israel found their identity in this story of God's blessing. For Jacob and for us, God's spoken word forms a community and demands a response. Faith is not personal and private; it is a communal response and responsibility.

*Read the remaining verses of Wesley's poem (*UMH *#387) that end with "thy nature, and thy name is love" to get his sense of Jacob's life-changing experience. What were the consequences of Jacob's experience for his family? for his people?*

Salvation by Faith

The themes of blessing and God's relationship to a community are also found in a sermon by John Wesley based on Ephesians 2:8: "For by grace you have been saved through faith, and this is not your own doing; it is the gift of God." Wesley preached the sermon "Salvation by Faith" on June 11, 1738, at St. Mary's Church in Oxford. It was the first sermon he had preached following his heart-warming experience at Aldersgate in late May of that year. One purpose behind Wesley's sermons was doctrinal instruction (*BOD*, par. 66, p. 51). We will be joining those who heard Wesley's sermon "Salvation by Faith" to explore images of God drawn from Wesley's interpretation of this passage from Ephesians. And we will examine Wesley's answers to our questions: Who is God? What has God done?

We cannot fully comprehend the importance of Wesley's understanding of God in this sermon without noting something of his journey in faith. Like Jacob, Wesley did not come to his relationship with God easily. His whole life was characterized by a struggle to understand faith and to be faithful.

Wesley's growth in faith began at childhood. With his brothers and sisters, he was trained at an early age about the meaning of faithful discipleship. Not only did the Wesley children learn Scripture and prayers and creeds, but they also were taught to tell the truth and to respect the privacy of others. Worship and a concern for the needs of others were part of their daily lives. The seeds of Wesley's understanding of *social holiness,* our response to God's love through our actions toward other persons and our need for accountability in community, were planted here.

When he went to Oxford, Wesley developed his disciplined spiritual life even further. Brother Charles had gathered a group of young men together to form the Holy Club, and John quickly became its leader. This group met regularly for study, prayer, and shared accountability for daily living. Their activities eventually expanded to prison ministry and counseling others in the faith.

But Wesley was already struggling with his basic faith question: "What must I do to be saved?" The question reflects his search for the meaning of faith and clarity about his relationship with God. Who God is, what God has done, and what God wants from us was at the heart of Wesley's faith struggle. Even in the midst of this struggle, Wesley was clear that he could not find the answers alone. His journals are full of accounts of relationships and experiences that helped shape his faith journey.

John Wesley's relationship with his mother, Susanna, was formative at all stages of his journey. While Wesley was at Oxford, he understood faith to be a matter of assenting to certain beliefs and living a disciplined life in obedience to God's will. John discussed this matter with his mother through an exchange of letters. He wrote:

> Faith is a species of belief, and belief is defined, an assent to a proposition upon rational grounds. Without rational grounds there is therefore no belief, and consequently no faith.[4]

Susanna Wesley's response came a month later. In her letter, she indicated her disagreement with John's definition of faith:

> You are somewhat mistaken in your notion of faith. All faith is an assent, but all assent is not faith. . . .
>
> The true measure of faith is the authority of the revealer, the weight of which always holds proportion with our conviction of his ability and integrity. Divine faith is an assent to whatever God has revealed to us, because [God] has revealed it.[5]

Susanna's reply indicates the importance of relationship with the one giving the revelation. God's truth carries the most power because of the nature and authority of God.

Take a few moments to write your definition of faith. How is your faith story similar to or different from Wesley's? What experiences have shaped your understanding of faith?

The discussion about the nature of faith with Susanna was not the end of Wesley's struggle with his relationship with God. He continued to practice a disciplined spiritual life in order to do God's will. But even Wesley's strict discipline was not enough. In 1736, a mission trip to Georgia resulted in a disastrous failure. Wesley had failed in his personal relationships and in his ministry. With his whole world falling apart, Wesley not only questioned his ability to do God's will, but doubted the validity of his faith as well.

On Wesley's return to England in 1738, he met a Moravian named Peter Böhler, a witness to what Wesley called "a living faith." Böhler, like Susanna Wesley, believed John Wesley was entirely too rational in his faith, leaving little room for God's grace. By April of 1738, on the teaching and insistence of Böhler, Wesley came to accept "a sure trust and confidence which a [person] hath in God, that through the merits of Christ *his* [or her] sins are forgiven, and *he* [or she] reconciled to the favour of God."[6] The happiness and holiness in the lives of Böhler and others who experienced this living faith were evident to Wesley. He finally admitted that his expectation of complete obedience to God's law was more than any human could do alone.[7]

It was only a short step for Wesley from realizing that faith is God's free gift to his own personal experience of repentance and assurance at a society meeting in Aldersgate Street. Wesley described the event:

> In the evening I went very unwillingly to a society in Aldersgate Street, where one was reading Luther's Preface to the Epistle to the Romans. About a quarter before nine, while he was describing the change which God works in the heart through faith in Christ, I felt my heart strangely warmed. I felt I did trust in Christ, Christ alone for salvation, and an assurance was given me that he had taken away *my* sins, even *mine,* and saved *me* from the law of sin and death.[8]

Aldersgate was not the end of John Wesley's faith journey. In many ways it was only the beginning, but it did bring him a new perspective on faith and a conviction of the great gift of God's grace. According to Robert Cushman, the working of God through the Holy Spirit is at the heart of John Wesley's understanding of salvation. At Aldersgate, Cushman writes, "[John Wesley] has personally *experienced* God's working, namely, a revolution of mind and a renovation of life."[9]

*Read the "Historical Statement" (*BOD, *pp. 9-11), which reflects the importance of Wesley's experience and its effects on his ministry. We have learned that Wesley's faith journey was very much shaped and shared in community, in relationship with others. As you think about the Historical Statement and the brief account of Wesley's faith journey* *here, identify some important relationships or experiences that affected Wesley's growth in faith.*

Then spend some time reflecting on how God has been at work in your life. God's action may have come through a specific event, or it may have been a lifelong process. What significant relationships or faith communities have contributed to your faith journey?

Wesley's sermon at St. Mary's was preached out of his newfound trust in God's grace. Even the title, "Salvation by Faith," reveals a shift from a totally rational to a more experiential understanding of God. Humans could do nothing to earn God's grace, which is freely given. Later Wesley would come to a more balanced view of God's grace and human response. But at this point in his faith journey, he was overwhelmed by the discovery that he could trust the forgiving nature of God's grace completely.

Wesley's sermon begins with a statement about God's blessing and a hidden reference to Jacob in the assertion that we have no claim to the least of God's mercies. To help us hear Wesley's meaning for our time more clearly, inclusive language has been substituted for exclusive language and enclosed within brackets in the following excerpt:

> 1. All the blessings which God hath bestowed upon [humans] are of [God's] mere grace, bounty, or favour: [God's] free, undeserved favour, favour altogether undeserved, [humanity] having no claim to the least of [God's] mercies. It was free grace that "formed [humans] of the dust of the ground, and breathed into [them] a living soul", and stamped on that soul the image of God, and "put all things under [their] feet". The same free grace continues to us, at this day, life, and breath, and all things. For there is nothing we are, or have, or do, which can deserve the least thing at God's hand. "All our works thou, O God, hast wrought in us." These therefore are so many more instances of free mercy: and whatever righteousness may be found in [humanity], this also is the gift of God.[10]

Once again we see the theme of God as the God of relationship. Wesley reminds us that faith is not private and personal. God creates us to be in community. We are in relationship to God, to one another, and to the world. And all that we are or do or have is from God.

Take some time to examine the beginning of this sermon for John Wesley's answers to our questions: Who is God? What has God done? How would you share Wesley's answers today with someone who has never been to church?

*Charles Wesley wrote a hymn based on Ephesians 2:8-10, "Let Us Plead for Faith Alone" (*UMH *#385). Sing or read this hymn to see how the message of "Salvation by Faith" is also communicated through a teaching hymn.*

John Wesley's sermon is based on a theme at the heart of his theology: that God acted *for us* through Jesus Christ and is now working *in us* through grace. Nothing that we do could merit God's mercy. God's act of saving grace is yet another manifestation of the blessing and covenant that God made with Jacob and his people.

Wesley specifically notes what he has learned about faith when he states that faith is not only a "speculative, rational thing," but also a "disposition of the heart."[11] It is trust in God who gives us everything. This God is portrayed through at least three different images in Wesley's sermon.

First, Wesley portrays the God we trust as an *"indulgent Father."* Through God's grace we are saved from guilt and "fear of punishment, from fear of the wrath of God, whom [we] now no longer regard as a severe master, but as an indulgent Father."[12] As God's children, we have received what Wesley calls "the Spirit of adoption." Our hope and our promise is that we will always be God's children—nothing can separate us from the love of God. Just as Jacob was forever bound to his father through Isaac's blessing, so also we are bound to God.

A second image for God is the *all powerful, almighty God.* Wesley tells us that the atonement of Christ has saved us from sin. When we are born anew in the faith, we continue to grow, "going on in the might of the Lord his God." The power of a God who named a people Israel is power enough to save all those who repent of their sin.

A *God of mercy and grace* is by far the most predominant image in Wesley's sermon. This image can be seen in the beginning paragraph: "For there is nothing we are, or have, or do, which can deserve the least thing at God's hand. 'All our works thou, O God, hast wrought in us.'" And all that we have or do are "instances of free mercy" from God's grace. Wesley returns again and again to this theme telling us that if we are "dead in sin," all we have to do is "return ye unto the Lord, and he will have mercy upon you, and to our God, [who] will abundantly pardon" (Isa. 55:7).[13]

Once we have repented of our sin, the God of grace will bless us with the greatest gift of all, salvation:

> If then sinful [persons] find favour with God, it is "grace upon grace." If God vouchsafe still to pour fresh blessings upon us—yea, the greatest of all blessings, salvation—what can we say to these things but "Thanks be unto God for [God's] unspeakable gift!"[14]

This blessing is a source of hope for Wesley, who remembers that there was mercy for members of the faith community who preceded him, such as Zacchaeus and Mary Magdalene. Out of this memory, Wesley realizes, "Then I, even I, may hope for mercy!"[15]

Take a few moments to step into John Wesley's shoes and answer these questions: Who is God? What has God done?

It is through our faith in a God of grace that we are saved. "Grace is the source, faith the condition, of salvation."[16] Just as God came to Jacob and his people in the night, so also a blessing is bestowed upon us unearned. God provides the means of salvation through Christ and now works within us so that we may repent and know this God of mercy and grace. And through God's blessing, we are all joined with Jacob and his people in covenant with God forever. We too become God's people. In the words of Charles Wesley:

> Come, let us use the grace divine, and all with one accord,
> in a perpetual covenant join ourselves to Christ the Lord;
> give up ourselves, thru Jesus' power, his name to glorify;
> and promise, in this sacred hour, for God to live and die.
> (*UMH* #606)

God's Blessing, Our Invitation

In the final section of this chapter dealing with the biblical witness to the nature of God, we will reflect together on how God's blessing becomes our invitation to discipleship. We will have an opportunity to answer the questions of who God is and what God has done out of our own faith experience.

God's blessing is an affirmation of a way of life, a call to discipleship. We have learned that God made a covenant with Jacob through a blessing that established Jacob as the leader of a people, Israel. God's blessing on Israel called for a new way of life, a new vocational identity. And we found that for John Wesley, God's greatest blessing is the gift of grace that provides for our salvation and demands our response.

Take some time to review what you have learned about the nature of God from our study of Jacob's faith journey and from John Wesley's sermon. What additional images of God have you discovered? Which images speak most deeply to you? why?

In the Gospel of Matthew, we are given a vision of what it is like to live under God's rule through the model of Jesus' life and ministry. Matthew asks the question, What will life be like under God's rule? One answer comes through Jesus' teachings in the Beatitudes, or blessings, which affirm the way of life of those who have already experienced God's saving grace. But these blessings also provide an opportunity for others to join in this life of discipleship. God guides the followers of Jesus in a particular way of life. Although God's reign is not yet present in full (see Matt. 12:28 and 4:17), we can feel its impact in the present by following God's guidance for our lives. In this way, we participate in the coming reign of God.

Read the series of blessings in Matthew 5:1-11 and answer these questions about the Beatitudes: Where does the Sermon on the Mount take place? Who is present? What is the purpose? What is Jesus doing? Who is speaking? Why would Jesus begin a sermon with a series of blessings?

Now look at the sequence that surrounds these blessings:

Matt. 4:17	*Jesus announces the presence of God's reign.*
Matt. 4:18-22	*Jesus calls disciples.*
Matt. 6:23	*Jesus preaches the gospel of the Kingdom.*
Matt. 5–7	*Jesus instructs the disciples about discipleship.*

Together we will examine the Beatitudes or blessings that begin the Sermon on the Mount to see what guidance they provide. Just as Jesus used these blessings to teach the disciples and others who were present, so also they teach us about discipleship. We will look at each Beatitude or blessing from two perspectives.

First, we will briefly reflect on the kind of life that is being affirmed in each blessing. The beginning of each Beatitude tells us how God wants us to live. It is important to notice that these blessings are plural in form. They are not addressed to an individual but to a people, the followers of Jesus. Second, we will think about the nature of the One who offers such a blessing through the promises that are made following each affirmation. The Beatitudes provide answers to our questions: Who is God? What has God done? What does God want from us?[17]

Blessed are the poor in spirit . . .

John Wesley's sermon has led us into the heart of this Beatitude through the idea that there is nothing we can do to merit God's grace. The word "poor" here means powerless and dependent. A common theme from the Hebrew Bible is God's protection and vindication of the poor. Those who give up their power to serve God in humility join the physically poor and dependent as recipients of this blessing. In other words, those who experience God's saving grace live a life of repentance (see Matt. 4:17) and service. God's claim on our lives is for us to put aside our self-centeredness and our materialism to become God's representatives on earth through our service to others.

. . . for theirs is the kingdom of heaven.

Jacob's experience taught us that God is a *God of promise*. The promise in this Beatitude is that living under God's rule leads us to the kingdom of heaven announced by Jesus (Matt. 4:17). Through Jesus' life and ministry on earth, we have a vision of what this new life can be as God's promise for the future is being fulfilled through Jesus. If we trust in God's saving presence, then God's promise to Jacob becomes our promise: "I am with you, I will keep you, I will bring you back to this land." Those who serve in humility and repentance will see the kingdom of heaven.

Blessed are those who mourn . . .

Those who mourn are not only persons who have lost loved ones but also those who see the brokenness of the world and work toward reconciliation. Fractured relationships are all around us in the separation of people from God, from people, and from the created world. This brokenness is manifest in loneliness and depression, in alienation from others, and in destruction of natural resources. Those who mourn protest against the oppression and injustice which lead to separation and alienation. This blessing affirms persons who choose to live out the story of God's grace through their actions toward others and the created world.

. . . for they will be comforted.

God has intervened in the world on our behalf by sending us God's own son, Jesus. The God who is present with us (see Matt. 1:23) is encountered in brokenness and weakness. Through the life and ministry of Jesus, God is revealed as a *God of healing*. We are reconciled to God through Jesus, and those who mourn because of loss or separation are comforted. God has promised to destroy sin and death and is already at work in the world to bless those who work for healing and reconciliation with our neighbors and the created world.

Blessed are the meek . . .

The meek are those who come to God utterly dependent and empty-handed. They follow Jesus' example by trusting God and obeying God's will for their lives. The meek do not use power to abuse the weak or to exploit nature. Participating in God's plan for reconciliation and wholeness is the sole aim of those who are meek. Their service is characterized by humility.

. . . for they will inherit the earth.

Under God's rule, the powerful will be brought down and the powerless will be raised up. The image of a *faithful and sustaining God* dominates this blessing. God is with the powerless, and in the end, they will triumph. "Inherit the earth" designates place, and our place gives us identity. Psalm 24:1 tells us "the earth is the LORD's," and to be part of God's place is our faith heritage. God's rule extends over God's world, and we know of God's faithfulness to God's promise to bless all the earth (Gen. 12:1-3). Under this rule, we are invited to claim our identity as disciples, obeying God's will for our lives. The promise of this blessing is that those who serve with humility will have a special place under God's rule.

Blessed are those who hunger and thirst for righteousness . . .

Hunger and thirst are basic physical needs of human beings. The words are used here as metaphors for a spiritual longing for God's saving presence in our lives. We are aware of the estrangement in our lives and our need for a right relationship with God. We need energy and discipline to do God's will. To be righteous means to be in relationship with God, and this relationship leads us to give up our self-centeredness in order to work for justice in the world.

. . . for they will be filled.

The promise of this blessing is that those who seek to live in relationship with God, participating in God's purpose of reconciliation and wholeness, will be satisfied in the doing of God's will. There is no need for satisfaction in materialism or individualism, in our career, or in doing our own thing. God will act on our behalf. The image of God here is one of the God within, the *God who empowers us* to be faithful, to do justice, and to walk humbly with our God (Mic. 6:8). As John Wesley taught, all that we are or do or have comes from God. Because of our inner relationship with God (inner piety), we are called and empowered to live our lives in love of our neighbor and the created world (social holiness).

Blessed are the merciful . . .

God's saving action comes to us freely through Jesus Christ. As Wesley repeatedly told us and Jacob certainly showed us, we can do nothing to earn God's mercy. Even when we seem the most unforgivable, God is merciful. God's compassion and concern for us is passed on to others as we live out of that same compassion and concern. Because God's mercy is available to all, we are called on to care for all persons and to exclude none. Through our acts of mercy, God becomes present for others.

. . . for they will receive mercy.

This Beatitude points toward the final judgment when we hope for mercy from God. The image of God here is of a *forgiving God, a God of mercy,* who has pardoned us for our sins through the life and ministry of Jesus Christ. As a community of disciples, we have received the gift of God's mercy and our life together should be a witness to that gift of God's accepting love (Matt. 18:21-35).

Blessed are the pure in heart . . .

Those who are pure in heart live a life focused on God. The one requirement for joining the early Methodist societies was an apt expression of this blessing: The goal is to sin no more, to live in commitment to God. The affirmation of Jesus' teaching here is that we purposely seek a different way of life built on goodness and honesty.

. . . for they will see God.

God is the One who claims us. Therefore, our lives must be centered on God's guidance. This is the *God of accountability* who sets our task before us. Samuel Wesley repeatedly told his son John, "God gives us our work," and "God will direct you."[18] God promised Jacob to be with him always, and that is our promise, too. Those who live a God-centered life will be rewarded by God's presence and guidance. The Jesus who announces these beatitudes is Emmanuel, "God with us" (Matt. 1:23).

Blessed are the peacemakers . . .

Peacemakers are loyal to God, above all. Peacemakers work not only for the absence of war, but also for the end of exploitation of persons and the created world. There can be no peace as long as people are homeless, hungry, or imprisoned. Peace is the ultimate result of God's rule when all shall live as brothers and sisters and care for one another.

. . . for they will be called children of God.

To live under God's rule as brothers and sisters is to share God's life. We must give up our reliance on self and depend wholly on God's saving grace. In this Beatitude, the image of God is a *God of freedom.* When we give up our determination to be in charge and rely on God, we experience a freedom from fear and anxiety, a freedom from competition with our neighbor, and a freedom from separation from our brothers and sisters. John Wesley told us that we have been adopted by God and we will always be God's children. That is the promise and our hope.

Blessed are those who are persecuted for righteousness' sake . . .
. . . for theirs is the kingdom of heaven.

The final two Beatitudes deal with the subject of persecution and warn us that the life-style we are about as disciples may not be popular with our peers. It is a warning of the consequences of living under God's rule now and a call to persevere. These blessings remind us of the role of the community of disciples in sustaining one another. It is in the faith community that God's sustaining presence is encountered. Persecution seems relatively unfamiliar to us in our time, although we may have experienced some social pressure to conform to the standards of others in our work or play. In truth, we probably have not known real persecution for living our faith. We do know that if the way of discipleship is not easy, we can rely on God to be with us. The image of God in these two Beatitudes is that of the *God who reigns* over all.

Now that we have briefly reviewed each Beatitude, select one for further reflection. Use Bible commentaries and a Bible dictionary to learn more about the Beatitude you have selected. How would you interpret the affirmation, "Blessed are . . ."? Then think about the meaning of this Beatitude for your life. How is it calling you to live?

The Beatitudes describe a way of life under God's rule for the followers of Jesus. In that sense, they become a source of accountability for us when we pray "thy kingdom come" (Matt. 6:10). We can measure our lives as disciples against what God affirms through Jesus' teaching in the Beatitudes.

In a similar way, John Wesley describes the characteristics or way of life for those who have experienced God's saving presence in a very specific way. "The Nature, Design, and General Rules of Our United Societies" (*BOD,* par. 67, pp. 71-73) gives explicit expectations for the life-style of Jesus' followers.

*Read John Wesley's general rules (*BOD, *pp. 71-73) and compare how they are related to the life-style defined by the Beatitudes. How do these guides (Beatitudes and Wesley's Rules) call us to accountability today?*

Our story of faith is a story of a God who acts through history in mercy and grace. God is the One who is always with us to guide us. God blessed Jacob with a new name and a new vocation as the leader of a people; God blessed John Wesley with unmerited grace; and God blesses us by traveling with us on our faith journeys. Sometimes we call to God, "Come, O thou Traveler unknown, whom still I hold, but cannot see!" And God's promise to Jacob rings in our ears, "I am with you, I will keep you, and I will bring you back to this land." Matthew repeats this promise: "And they shall name him Emmanuel, which means, 'God is with us'" (Matt. 1:23); "For where two or three are gathered in my name, I am there among them" (Matt. 18:20); "And remember, I am with you always, to the end of the age" (Matt. 28:20). God's assurance of blessing demands our response. How will we live as faithful disciples?

CHAPTER THREE

'Tis Love! 'Tis Love!

Our Inherited Witness

OUR STUDY OF THE BIBLICAL WITNESS HAS REVEALED A GOD OF MERCY AND GRACE, A GOD WHO BLESSES US AND CLAIMS US AS GOD'S OWN. With Jacob, through the words of Charles Wesley, we affirmed:

'Tis Love! 'tis Love! thou diedst for me,
I hear thy whisper in my heart.
The morning breaks, the shadows flee,
pure Universal Love thou art:
to me, to all, thy mercies move—
thy nature, and thy name is Love.
(*UMH* #387)

The biblical witness to the God of grace who loves us and calls us to faithful discipleship is echoed through tradition, our inherited witness.

Our tradition or history is the faith community's account of the continuing experience of being God's people. The story of our heritage in faith is a record of God's covenant with a community. It is an account of how God has acted on our behalf in history and how persons of faith have responded with lives of love and service. Our tradition is a story that gives us identity; it names who we are as God's people.

We have learned that across time, people of faith have reflected about who God is and what God has done. From the beginning, the people of the early church had questions as they thought about the relationship between God and Jesus. Could God really take human form in Jesus Christ? If so, could Jesus be fully human and fully divine? Could God suffer through Jesus' suffering? In each new generation, Christians have tried to find ways to talk about what God has done, but there are still questions.

Throughout the chapter we will consider God's inner being, or the relationships between the persons of the Trinity—God, Jesus Christ, and the Holy Spirit. At issue is the way in which we understand who God is and what God has done. Even in the midst of our study and reflection, we remember that we can never fully understand God, that God is mystery. But we do know that God is relational and has chosen to relate to us in different ways as Trinity.

In this chapter we will use *tradition* as a way to help us understand the nature of God by studying historical perspectives on the Trinity. Statements of faith about who God is and what God has done will help us reflect on the relationships between God, Christ, and Holy Spirit. In the first part of the chapter, we will examine the language used for the persons of the Trinity, second-century to fifth-century debates about the nature of God, and the statements of faith formulated as creeds.

In the second part of the chapter, we will turn to the historical documents of The United Methodist Church that provide our doctrinal standards: "The Articles of Religion" from The Methodist Church and the "Confession of Faith" from The Evangelical United Brethren Church. We will see what they teach us about the triune nature of God.

Finally, we will examine the understanding of God in a covenanting statement from the Consultation on Church Union. This document has been recognized by our General Conference of The United Methodist Church and is a result of our denomination's participation in an ecumenical dialogue toward Christian unity.

In each part of the chapter, we will use the same method of study. We will begin by looking at the historical circumstances or how the documents came to be written. Next, we will examine the understanding of God as Trinity reflected in the documents. And then we will turn to what these documents mean for our own lives of discipleship and our faith community.

Language: Debates About the Nature of God

As we study the Trinity, we need to pay particular attention to the language used to express the nature of the triune God across the centuries. How we talk about God reveals what we are thinking about God. How do we talk about a God who is known in different ways? Father, Son, and Holy Ghost is a traditional formula, but we may also use Father, Son, and Holy Spirit; or God, Christ, and Spirit. Creator, Redeemer, and Sustainer is a common formulation, but some may prefer Creating, Redeeming, and Sustaining God (or the One who creates, redeems, and sustains) as a way to express the continuing work of a triune God who is active in the world. Another way of talking about the Trinity is to see God as the One beyond us, the One among us, and the One within us.

Take a few moments to reflect on your own understanding of God and what you know or believe about God in three persons. Then jot down any questions you have about the Trinity. Are you more comfortable in your relationship with one person of the Trinity than another?

Now take a few moments to list some of your favorite names for the persons of the Trinity. For example, many find the term "Loving Parent" meaningful when addressing God in prayer.

As Christians, we use a variety of names and images for the persons of the Trinity. Each of these expressions attempts to help us understand a relational God who is known to us in different ways—the One who loves us and who chooses to be in relationship with us.

*Read the first "Basic Christian Affirmation" (*BOD, *par. 65, p. 42) and think about the understanding of the triune God you find there. A hymn that reflects some of the ways God relates to us is "Creating God, Your Fingers Trace" (Jeffery Rowthorn;* UMH *#109). Sing or read the hymn and consider what the words mean to you in light of your own faith experience.*

The formulation of the Trinity as we know it is not found in Scripture, but the New Testament writers do refer to all three persons of the Trinity. Writers differ in the emphasis they place on the actions of the three. For example, Father-Son and Son-Spirit relationships are referred to in the Gospel of John, but not the relationship between all three. And Paul ends the second letter to the Corinthians with a blessing: "The grace of the Lord Jesus Christ, the love of God, and the communion of the Holy Spirit be with all of you" (2 Cor. 13:13). Although Paul names the three persons of the Trinity, he does not discuss how the three relate to one another. Ephesians refers to the three persons, but emphasizes the oneness of God: "There is one body and one Spirit, just as you were called to the one hope of your calling, one Lord, one faith, one baptism, one God and Father of all, who is above all and through all and in all" (Eph. 4:4-6). Matthew also names three persons, but doesn't say anything about how the three work together in baptism: "Go therefore and make disciples of all nations, baptizing them in the name of the Father and of the Son and of the Holy Spirit" (Matt. 28:19).

It was left to the early church to interpret the interrelationships of the Trinity. Donald McKim writes:

> What emerged from reflection on the New Testament as a whole was a growing realization of the relationships between God, Jesus Christ, and the Holy Spirit; how these three are related was a source of discussion and debate for many years. From the New Testament comes the strong sense that to answer who God is requires Christians to affirm God not only as one but also three.[1]

Out of its reflection on the New Testament, the early church formulated the concept of the Trinity as an interpretation of Scripture to help us know who God is and what God has done.

The Creeds: Early Statements of Faith

Each of the documents we are studying is the result of the faith community's reflection about the nature of God and our relationship with God. The results of the church's reflection are preserved in creeds and confessions of faith. K. James Stein of Garrett-Evangelical Seminary discusses a helpful distinction between these two forms of faith expression made by H. M. DuBose of the Methodist Episcopal Church, South, in 1907:

DuBose performed the useful service of drawing the distinction between creeds (those fixed statements of faith which express the catholicity of the church in terms of all the basic Christian beliefs, e.g., the Apostles' Creed) and confessions (those more Protestant expressions emerging in the sixteenth century, which were adopted in order to protest heresy or to justify a new denomination's existence).[2]

We will be looking at creeds from the early church in this part of the chapter and confessions in the following United Methodist and COCU sections.

A Heated Debate

After Jesus' death, much of the early debate was about how to understand God in light of the incarnation, death, and resurrection of Jesus Christ. Could God really take human form and walk among us, die, and be resurrected? Is God the Creator the same as or different from God the Redeemer? These questions about God were at the heart of the early church's struggle to be faithful, and they are questions that have been asked anew in each generation.

In the second century, Irenaeus became one of the earliest theologians to state his understanding of how God is manifested in Jesus. Irenaeus emphasized an indwelling God described by Paul: "I have been crucified with Christ; and it is no longer I who live, but it is Christ who lives in me. And the life I now live in the flesh I live by faith in the Son of God, who loved me and gave himself for me" (Gal. 2:19*b*-20). Irenaeus also affirmed the goodness of creation, believing that humans were created with the capacity for both goodness and immortality. But both goodness and immortality were lost through sin and were recovered only through God's work in Christ Jesus, who was "God incarnate in human form, the full revelation of God."[3]

Irenaeus recognized God's transcendence (otherness), but he chose to emphasize God's immanence (indwelling presence). He used relational images of God as shepherd or father to talk about how God acts in history to care for us. For Irenaeus, the importance of the Trinity was not so much how the persons of the Trinity relate to one another, but how God chooses different ways to relate to humanity, particularly in Jesus. God is actively involved in the world, not distant and inaccessible.

How do you talk about your relationship with God? What images do you use to share your belief in the Trinity? Look at some of the hymns dealing with the theme "Trinity" to see what words and images the writers used to talk about their belief in the Trinity (see "Index of Topics and Categories," UMH, *p. 953).*

The debate about who God is did not end with the affirmations of Irenaeus. Those who were faithful were still reflecting on who God is and what God has done. The First General Council of the church met in Nicea in May, 325 C.E. Three hundred bishops were present and adopted the Nicene Creed as a united expression of faith. (A helpful analysis of the Nicene Creed can be found in *DSTT*, 17.)

The Nicene Creed affirms a belief in one God: "We believe in one God, the Father, the Almighty, maker of heaven and earth, of all that is, seen and unseen" (*UMH* #880). This is a belief Christians share with their Jewish sisters and brothers. In the Hebrew Bible, we find the Jewish affirmation of faith, the *Shema:* "Hear, O Israel: The LORD our God is one LORD" (Deut. 6:4 KJV). This God is the hidden, awesome, holy God who challenged Jacob throughout the night. The Creator God of the Hebrew Bible is the One who made a covenant with Jacob and called a people to be God's people. This God is the One who creates us, who blesses us, and who claims us, giving us our identity and our vocation.

The Nicene Creed was also a result of the New Testament witness to the nature of God. In the process of reflection, the early Christians began to recognize that the New Testament reveals that God is made known to us through God's work in Jesus Christ and God's continuing presence through the Holy Spirit. But, as Donald McKim writes, the process of reflection and naming who God is took a long time:

> Such a complicated and important theological problem as God's identity obviously requires careful thought and expression. . . . From the start, however, certain basic tenets were accepted: (1) God is one and not two or three gods as in pagan religions; (2) God is revealed in three ways as

> Father, Son, and Holy Spirit; (3) the Father and the Son are distinct from each other and thus should not be equated so as to erase differences between them.[4]

Following more than fifty years of continued debate about how God, Christ, and the Holy Spirit are related, a second Nicene Council met in Constantinople in 381 C.E. and refined the Creed to lengthen the statement about Jesus Christ and to include the statement on the Holy Spirit. This is the creed we now use in worship in The United Methodist Church (*UMH* #880). In coming to this decision, the Council rejected many interpretations that had been suggested in the continuing debate, such as: (1) Christ was a created being, subordinate to God, and one of God's helpers; (2) Jesus Christ was divine, but appeared to be human; (3) Jesus Christ was human, but appeared to be divine; (4) the Holy Spirit was one of God's helpers and not of the same substance as God; and (5) the Trinity was made up of three different persons with three different roles.

Although the debate contained many intricate theological issues, the Nicene Council was able to conclude its deliberations with a statement affirming that a real relationship exists between God and Jesus Christ, who share the same divine nature:

> We believe in one Lord, Jesus Christ,
> the only Son of God,
> eternally begotten of the Father,
> God from God, Light from Light,
> true God from true God,
> begotten, not made,
> of one Being with the Father . . .
> (*UMH* #880)

And the same is true of the Holy Spirit, who is in relationship with God and of the same nature:

> We believe in the Holy Spirit, the Lord, the giver of life,
> who proceeds from the Father . . .
> (*UMH* #880)

The persons of the Trinity share the same divine nature. The Son is a different person from the Father, but is still God. The Spirit is a different person from the Father and the Son, but is still God. The persons of the Trinity always act with one accord and never disagree.

*Read the Nicene Creed (*UMH *#880). What can you learn about the nature of the Trinity and the relationships between the three persons of the Trinity? What images of God are used in this great statement of faith? Compare the descriptive words and images in the Nicene Creed with those found in "We Believe in One True God" (Tobias Clausnitzer; see* UMH *#85).*

Councils of the church continued to meet throughout the fourth and fifth centuries to work on the theological questions about the nature of God and what God had done in Christ and continues to do in the Holy Spirit. What is now known as the Fourth Ecumenical Council met in Chalcedon in 451 C.E. The conclusion of the Chalcedon Creed is usually seen as the "orthodox" solution to the christological problem: "Chalcedon affirmed both the distinction and the completeness of Jesus Christ as being God and a human being at the same time."[5] This council affirmed that the Trinity exists simultaneously. God is always one God in three forms. Christ is truly God and truly human. The Spirit is truly God and truly Spirit. So the persons of the Trinity make God known to us in different ways:

> The doctrine of the Trinity is an attempt to describe the indescribable. Yet God is known in and through the created order. God is known and experienced in the historic Jesus and the risen Christ. And God is known and experienced as a presence that sustains, inspires, guides, and empowers. God, in God's own being and essence, contains unity amid diversity and mystery amid revelation. (*DSTTLG,* 19)

The Meaning for Us

We find in the Nicene Creed an affirmation of faith about who God is and what God has done. This statement is part of our tradition, the inherited witness of God's people. The Nicene Creed reveals God's great love for us by portraying God as the One who creates, a loving

Parent who made all that is. God also came to us as the One who redeems, the One among us who became human, died, and rose again for our sake. And God is the One who sustains us, the One within us who spoke through the prophets and who speaks through us.

Sing or read "God Hath Spoken by the Prophets" (George W. Briggs; UMH *#108) and notice the descriptions of God, Christ Jesus, and the Spirit, as well as the emphasis on the oneness of God.*

Affirmations of faith are statements that shape a people. They name who we are as Christians, and they teach us about our doctrinal tradition. Affirming our faith is part of a continuing process of reflecting on the Good News of God's grace for every generation. We join Christians around the world in reciting these traditional creeds as a way to name God's relationship with us. Notice that the Nicene Creed states, "We believe." It is a response of a community to what God has done. A creed affirms that we are God's people called to be in relationship with God and with one another. Norman Madsen writes, "When we look at God, we see a perfect model of relationships and belonging for our everyday world. God is only God in the relationship of being Father, Son, and Holy Spirit. This godly model tells us that we are only human in our relatedness."[6]

Examine the affirmations of faith in the United Methodist Hymnal, *beginning with "The Apostles' Creed" (*UMH *#881) through "The World Methodist Social Affirmation" (*UMH *#886). Note the affirmations the creeds make about God, Christ, and Holy Spirit. How are the relationships between the persons of the Trinity described? Which creed holds the most meaning for you? why? Did you find any new images of God to add to your list?*

The Doctrinal Standards of The United Methodist Church

The historical documents that shape the identity of The United Methodist Church also emphasize a triune God. These statements of faith about who God is and what God has done serve as doctrinal standards for a denomination that believes the "gospel [is] grounded in the biblical message of God's self-giving love revealed in Jesus Christ" (*BOD*, par. 66, p. 49).

A Heritage of Faith

Church history is an account of the faith experience of a people and evidence of shared identity. Telling the story of our faith experience is our way of doing theology, of affirming our faith. Russell Richey writes, "So we Methodists do theology in our own way. And one way we do theology is by telling our story, the narrative of God's work in us and among us."[7]

*We could also say that United Methodists do theology by singing and praying our story. Sing or read Charles Wesley's hymn "Maker, in Whom We Live" (*UMH *#88) and examine the understanding of the Trinity he expresses. Also notice the names for the persons of the Trinity.*

Look in the United Methodist Hymnal *and* Book of Worship *for other hymns and prayers that express the meaning of the Trinity. In what ways is the Trinitarian formula used in acts of worship?*

The identity of The United Methodist Church has been shaped by its heritage—through the faithful witness of the early church, the affirmations of the church councils, the work of the reformers, and denominational expressions of faith. The union of Methodist and Evangelical United Brethren churches brought together traditions that shared similar historical and spiritual backgrounds, but spoke different languages (*BOD,* p. 7). Churches in both of these traditions adopted doctrinal statements early.

John Wesley sent the *Methodist* "Articles of Religion" (*BOD,* par. 67, pp. 58-65) to help with the organization of the new Methodist Church in America. "The Articles of Religion" and *The Sunday Service,* a simplified form of the English *Book of Common Prayer,* were adopted when The Methodist Episcopal Church was organized by the Christmas Conference in 1784. By this action, "The Articles of Religion" were established as basic norms for Christian belief. "American Methodists were not required to subscribe to the Articles after the Anglican manner, but they were accountable (under threat of trial) for keeping their proclamation of the gospel within the boundaries outlined therein" (*BOD,* par. 66, p. 52).

The Evangelical United Brethren Church had its roots in the spiritual awakening of the eighteenth and early nineteenth centuries. This awakening emphasized a vital relationship with God, who could be known through religious experience. Two churches united in 1946 to form this denomination: The United Brethren in Christ and The Evangelical Association.

In the eighteenth century, Philip Otterbein and Martin Boehm proclaimed a God of grace through "the Good News of God's redeeming mercy and love as demonstrated in Jesus Christ" (1988 *BOD,* p. 11). Their ministry among neglected German-speaking settlers of the Middle Colonies brought an invitation to accept God's saving grace, and salvation brought a personal commitment to Jesus Christ (1988 *BOD,* p. 11). As the work of Otterbein and Boehm expanded, the United Brethren in Christ held their organizing General Conference in 1815 and adopted their first "Confession of Faith" the same year.[8] In the early 1800s, Jacob Albright also focused on religion as a personal, conscious, experiential relationship with God. His ministry was to German-speaking people in Pennsylvania (*BOD,* p. 11). A movement that began with three small groups of people who covenanted to live a holy life grew into the Evangelical Association. Conversion was a central theme and purpose for the ministry of this church. Conversion was "a word which signified the gracious, conscious vitalization of the life of a person by an act of God" (1988 *BOD,* p. 13). The Evangelical Association adopted a German translation of "The Articles of Religion" in 1809 with only a few changes.[9]

The union of The Methodist and The Evangelical United Brethren Churches in 1968 brought together two spiritual traditions who were united in their belief that "Christian faith and experience ought to be expressed in holy living" (1988 *BOD,* p. 17). With the union came two foundational documents, which have served as doctrinal standards for The United Methodist Church: "The Articles of Religion" and the "Confession of Faith."

As you reflect on your reading of the historical documents in the Book of Discipline *(pp. 9-20), what did you find that surprised you, that was a new idea to you, that challenged you?*

Foundational Documents

Both the Methodist "Articles of Religion" and the Evangelical United Brethren "Confession of Faith" were accepted as doctrinal standards for The United Methodist Church in the 1968 Plan of Union. These historical documents connect us to centuries of reflection about who God is and what God has done. In the "Articles of Religion" and the "Confession of Faith," we are united with the apostolic tradition, the early church councils, the Protestant reformers, and our own denominational heritage. And through study of these doctrinal standards, we can gain new insights about who God is and what God has done. (For further study of the "Articles of Religion" and "Confession of Faith," see *TWBM* and *DSTT*.) We will look together at the understanding of the nature of God as Trinity contained in each of these documents in order to deepen our own faith and commitment to the One who creates, redeems, and sustains us.

"The Articles of Religion" and the "Confession of Faith" are statements of faith that "unite us with the historic faith of Christendom" (1988 *BOD*, p. 10). They function as a confession of what is central to our United Methodist identity and provide the clearest statement of our denominational understanding of who God is and what God has done.

The Articles of Religion

Article I.—Of Faith in the Holy Trinity

There is but one living and true God, everlasting, without body or parts, of infinite power, wisdom, and goodness; the maker and preserver of all things, both visible and invisible. And in unity of this Godhead there are three persons, of one substance, power, and eternity—the Father, the Son, and the Holy Ghost. (*BOD*, par. 67, pp. 58-59)

Confession of Faith

Article I.—God

We believe in the one true, holy and living God, Eternal Spirit, who is Creator, Sovereign and Preserver of all things visible and invisible. He is

> infinite in power, wisdom, justice, goodness and love, and rules with gracious regard for the well-being and salvation of men, to the glory of his name. We believe the one God reveals himself as the Trinity: Father, Son, and Holy Spirit, distinct but inseparable, eternally one in essence and power. (*BOD,* par. 67, p. 66)

Note all the words that are used by both confessions to name who God is and what God has done. Then make separate lists of the descriptive words that are unique to "The Articles of Religion" and the "Confession of Faith." Write a statement of faith about the Trinity in your own words.

It is clear that both of these confessions share the belief that God is one in three "distinct, but inseparable" persons. Shared descriptors of God include "true, living, infinite power, wisdom, goodness, and preserver." Notice in Article 1 of the Confession that the Trinity is also named "Creator, Sovereign and Preserver." Both these articles

> attempt to tell us who God is in God's very being. According to the Scriptures, God is made known in three persons—Father, Son, and Holy Ghost. So we are also dealing with relationships within God. No wonder early Christians struggled to understand the totality of God, and many of us still do. (*TWBM,* 15)

The Meaning for Us

At issue in the current discussion about the foundational documents of The United Methodist Church is the question about what authority these doctrinal standards carry for us. In other words, how are these corporate statements about who God is and what God has done related to what we believe as individuals or congregations? There are those like the late Albert Outler who believe that these landmark documents "remain essentially that—defining our heritage and giving us a basis upon which to address the contemporary crises—using as we do so the fourfold Wesleyan guidelines for determining truth."[10] Others, notably

Robert E. Cushman, believe these documents should be considered "positive, juridical norms of doctrine."[11]

Cushman asks what kind of stability can be expected of a church whose doctrinal standards are considered to be no more than "landmark documents" and whose doctrine seems to be a continuing process of "informed theological experimentation" and "never-ending tasks of theologizing."[12] "Our Doctrinal History" (*BOD,* par. 66, pp. 49-58) describes the issues in light of historical developments. Recent discussions about the place of developing theologies within the life of the church and the nature of our ecumenical relationships led to our current stance:

> The task of defining the scope of our Wesleyan tradition in the context of the contemporary world includes much more than formally reaffirming or redefining standards of doctrine, although these tasks may also be involved. The heart of our task is to reclaim and renew the distinctive United Methodist doctrinal heritage, which rightly belongs to our common heritage as Christians, for the life and mission of the whole Church today. (*BOD,* par. 66, p. 54)

With the renewed interest in reclaiming our Wesleyan heritage, the question about the authority of our doctrinal statements is still debated.

K. James Stein believes these foundational documents of the church are a link to the historic and universal church and names the value of the foundational documents for our lives of faith: (1) They are interpretations of the meaning of Scripture, (2) they unite us with historic church tradition, (3) they provide us with a foundation for thinking about who God is and what God has done, (4) they are grounds for dialogue with other theologies, and (5) they are a source for spiritual growth.[13]

However we view the value of our doctrinal standards, we cannot deny their central focus on a God who loves us enough to relate to us in different ways. We can never be separated from the One beyond us, the One among us, and the One within us. God, through love, has claimed us.

An Ecumenical Covenant

Our Wesleyan heritage includes a history of awareness of our unity with all Christians. After describing the distinctive marks of a Methodist in "The Character of a Methodist," John Wesley wrote:

> By these marks, by these fruits of a living faith, do we labour to distinguish ourselves from the unbelieving world, from all those whose minds or lives are not according to the Gospel of Christ. But from real Christians, of whatsoever denomination they be, we earnestly desire not to be distinguished at all, not from any who sincerely follow after what they know they have not yet attained. No: "Whosoever doeth the will of my Father which is in heaven, the same is my brother, and sister, and mother."[14]

The United Methodist Church continues this ecumenical tradition through the recognition of our common heritage with all Christians (*BOD,* par. 65, p. 40). With our brothers and sisters in the faith, we share some basic Christian affirmations (*BOD,* par. 65, pp. 42-43). The first affirmation indicates our common belief in the Trinity:

> **With Christians of other communions we confess belief in the triune God—Father, Son, and Holy Spirit.** This confession embraces the biblical witness to God's activity in creation, encompasses God's gracious self-involvement in the dramas of history, and anticipates the consummation of God's reign.
>
> The created order is designed for the well-being of all creatures and as the place of human dwelling in covenant with God. As sinful creatures, however, we have broken that covenant, become estranged from God, wounded ourselves and one another, and wreaked havoc throughout the natural order. We stand in need of redemption. (*BOD,* par. 65, p. 42)

This affirmation describes God's activity as Creator ("God's activity in creation"), Redeemer ("God's gracious self-involvement"), and Sustainer ("anticipates . . . God's reign"). It names our human sinfulness in breaking God's covenant and the resulting estrangement from God and one another. We need the reconciliation that comes through God's redeeming grace through Jesus Christ.

The History

It is through this understanding of our common Christian heritage that The United Methodist Church has participated in continuing ecumenical dialogue. Beginning in 1962, representatives from nine denominations along with observers and consultants began meeting to work toward a goal of being one in Christ. Several denominations are participating in the Consultation on Church Union, including the African Methodist Episcopal Church, African Methodist Episcopal Zion Church, Christian Church (Disciples of Christ), Christian Methodist Episcopal Church, Episcopal Church, International Council of Community Churches, Presbyterian Church (U.S.A.), United Church of Christ, and the United Methodist Church. Observers and consultants come from the Lutheran Council in the U.S.A., the Reformed Church in America, and the Roman Catholic Church.[15]

The United Methodist Church has been part of this search to find agreement on central theological issues in the life of the church. A full Plan of Union was presented in 1970 to participating churches, but it was clear that members of the Consultation "were not ready to enter into full and organic church union."[16] But the denominations did not want to end the dialogue toward such a union, so in 1973 they "began the process of living our way toward unity through shared study and action."[17]

The participating denominations agree that division in the church is a contradiction of its nature as the body of Christ. So they have made a commitment to one another to work toward being a "visibly united church."

> The goal of this process is to let our participating churches become one in the essentials of faith, worship, order, and witness. At the same time, it allows the churches to recognize and embrace the gifts of continued diversity our churches bring in their particular traditions, ethos, and racial and ethnic heritage, while we are spiritually renewed through these relationships and commitments.[18]

One result of this mutual process is the claiming of documents. *The COCU Consensus: In Quest of a Church of Christ Uniting* was recognized by the 1988 General Conference of The United Methodist Church as "an expression in the matters with which it deals, of the apostolic faith, order, worship, and witness of the church" (*BOR*, p. 206).

The Covenant

The *COCU Consensus* document is a "formal recognition by the participating churches of their respective members, churches, and ministries."[19] The sixteenth plenary of the Consultation adopted the resolution that names three purposes of the document:

> RESOLVED: that the 16th (1984) Plenary of the Consultation on Church Union approves this text and asks the participating churches, by formal action, to recognize in it
> 1) an expression, in the matters with which it deals, of the Apostolic faith, order, worship, and witness of the Church,
> 2) an anticipation of the Church Uniting which the participating bodies, by the power of the Holy Spirit, wish to become, and
> 3) a sufficient theological basis for the covenanting acts and the uniting process proposed at this time by the Consultation.[20]

The theological basis of the COCU document is deeply rooted in our shared historical tradition. In light of our study of the creeds, it is interesting to note that the *COCU Consensus* includes statements about the creeds, including: (8) "The Church Uniting will acknowledge the Apostles' Creed and the Nicene (Constantinopolitan) Creed as unique, ecumenical witnesses of Tradition to the revelation of God recorded in Scripture,"[21] and (9) "The Church Uniting will use these creeds in worship as acts of praise and allegiance to the Triune God, thus binding itself to the apostolic faith of the one Church in all centuries and continents."[22]

Frequent use of Trinitarian language is evident in the *COCU Consensus* throughout discussions of membership, confessing the faith, worship, and ministry. In section 5, "Confessing the Faith," the Covenant reads:

> 1) The Church lives and finds its identity in thankful confession of Jesus Christ as the one Lord and Savior (Col. 1:15-20). In Christ God's purpose for humanity is effectively made known (Eph. 1:9-10). Christ is God's self-giving in the Holy Spirit to be the life of the people of God (Jn. 1:4; Rom. 8:2). Christ therefore is "our wisdom, our righteousness and sanctification and redemption" (1 Cor. 1:30). Being justified by the faith in Christ, we are reconciled to God and to one another through the faith and love which is bestowed in the Spirit (2 Cor. 5:18-19; 1 Cor. 13). The Church thus confesses and worships in glad celebration the one triune God (Matt. 28:19; 2 Cor. 13:14).[23]

As you read this statement, what is the understanding of the triune God that is communicated? What can we learn about the relationship of the three persons of God? How does this understanding compare with the statements about the Trinity in the foundational documents of The United Methodist Church and the creeds?

This statement affirms that God's purpose for God's people was made known through Christ. We learned in chapter 2 that God's purpose for us was made known through the life and ministry of Jesus Christ. And through Jesus' teachings in the Beatitudes, we were given a vision of what it would be like to live under God's rule. Because God has chosen to relate to us in different ways as the One who creates us, the One who redeems us, and the One who sustains us, we can be reconciled with God and with one another.

The Meaning for Us

Our ecumenical dialogue about who God is and what God has done is part of our tradition and is in tune with Wesley's own interest in ecumenical discussion. The *Book of Discipline* states that "United Methodists share a common heritage with Christians of every age and nation. This heritage is grounded in the apostolic witness to Jesus Christ as Savior and Lord, which is the source and measure of all valid Christian teaching" (*BOD,* par. 65, pp. 40-41). Ecumenical dialogue reflects our participation in the larger Christian fellowship and challenges us to look beyond our own church toward the world community of faith.

We have experienced the richness of the diversity of sharing within our church and received new insights that have deepened our own faith. This same richness is available to us through sharing our faith with our Christian brothers and sisters. We gain clarity about our own understanding of God when we engage in dialogue with persons of other faiths. The discussion pushes us to know our own beliefs and our Wesleyan tradition so that we can communicate its distinctive nature more clearly.

Finally, our movement toward reunion with our Christian brothers and sisters leads us into the future. The vision of our shared heritage in faith moves us forward toward the time when we will all be one under God's rule.

CHAPTER FOUR

Through Faith I See Thee Face to Face

The Evidence of Faith

WE HAVE BEEN JOURNEYING TOGETHER IN FAITH AS WE STUDY OUR BELIEF IN GOD. In each chapter, we have used the four sources and criteria of the Wesleyan quadrilateral (Scripture, tradition, experience, and reason) to reflect on who God is and what God has done. We have also focused specifically on the biblical witness *(Scripture)* to God's blessing in chapter 2, and on the historic witness *(tradition)* to the triune God in creeds and confessions in chapter 3. Now we come to examine what God, the One who creates, redeems, and sustains, has done and is doing in our lives and in the life of our church *(experience)*.

Our own journeys of faith undoubtedly bear some similarity to those of Jacob, the early Christians, and John Wesley. Sometimes the journey has not been easy, but we have come to know that God is with us. God is a God of relationship who has chosen to be in covenant with God's people and has promised to be with us and to stay with us on the journey. We, too, can sing with joy:

> My prayer hath power with God; the grace
> unspeakable I now receive;
> through faith I see thee face to face,
> I see thee face to face, and live!
> In vain I have not wept and strove—
> Thy nature, and thy name is Love.
> (Charles Wesley; *UMH* #387)

God has been faithful to God's people in the past, God is present with us now, and God will journey with us into the future. Our journey with God is described by the *Book of Discipline* as both personal and corporate:

> On the personal level, experience is to the individual as tradition is to the Church; it is the personal appropriation of God's forgiving and empowering grace. Experience authenticates in our own lives the truths revealed in Scripture and illumined in tradition, enabling us to claim the Christian witness as our own. . . .
>
> Although profoundly personal, Christian experience is also corporate; our theological task is informed by the experience of the Church and by the common experiences of all humanity. In our attempts to understand the biblical message, we recognize that God's gift of liberating love embraces the whole of creation. (*BOD,* par. 68, pp. 80-81)

Our personal faith experience interacts with the community's witness from Scripture and tradition about who God is and what God has done and what God is doing. We have seen how the faith experience of Jacob's relationship with God reflects a nation's struggle with faith and how early Christians united in their affirmations of a God who is made known to us through the Trinity. We know the faith experience of John Wesley, Philip Otterbein, and Jacob Albright shaped a denomination. And ecumenical discussions about shared beliefs are leading the church into wholeness as the body of Christ. So, too, our own spiritual journeys affect the faith community at the same time they are being shaped by those with whom we worship.

In this part of our study about who God is and what God is doing, we will focus on God as the *author of salvation.* In the first part of the chapter, we will turn to the Gospel of Luke for clues to the nature of a God who invites us to a new relationship. Through our study of John Wesley's understanding of *via salutis* (the way of salvation) in the second section, we will examine our belief in the One who provides the way to salvation. And finally, we will reflect on God at work in our daily living as we consider John Wesley's understanding of personal piety and social holiness. Throughout this chapter we will be thinking about the different ways God relates to us as our Creator, Redeemer, and Sustainer.

God's Invitation

The Gospel Feast

God is our Creator, the One beyond us, who made us and chooses to be in relationship with us. With God, the door to relationship is always open and the banquet table is ready for us. God's invitation is evident in Jesus' parable of the gospel feast.

Read Luke 14:16-23 and think about your impressions of this parable. Look at what happened in verses 1-15 and consider what Jesus is trying to teach through this story. Do some further research in your Bible dictionary and commentaries. What questions does this parable raise for you?

It was the custom in the Jewish tradition for a host to issue an invitation to dinner in advance and then a second invitation when the meal was prepared: "Come; for everything is ready now" (Luke 14:17). In the parable from Luke, the servant went out to notify those who were to be guests, but complications arose. Fred Craddock, homiletics professor and noted preacher, observes that the excuses made by those who were first invited were common and would have been honored in their society: "The forces against which God's offer contends are reasonable and well argued, but God's offer has priority not simply over our worst, but also our best agendas."[1] When the invitation came, some had legitimate excuses and could not attend. Up to this point, Jesus told a familiar story. There were no surprises for the hearers. But the rest of the story provides a shocking turn of events.

The second guest list is unexpected and somewhat inconceivable: "the poor, the crippled, the blind, and the lame." And when there was still more room at the feast, the host sent his servant out to invite travelers from the "roads and lanes" to come to the table as well. The second guest list invites those who were normally forbidden access to such meals in Jewish society—persons with handicapping conditions and foreign travelers, likely to be Gentiles or persons from foreign places.[2]

And the outcasts of society accepted the invitation to fellowship.

It does not take a great leap of the imagination to think of God as the host in this parable and the banquet as a metaphor for God's rule. Under God's rule, all who seek a relationship with God share God's life-giving food. In this parable, "Jesus reveals a God who 'eats with,' shares life with society's handicapped and declares a person righteous who does the same."[3] God's gospel feast brought together the unexpected, the "poor in spirit." Those who accepted God's invitation to relationship were the outcasts of their society.

Imagine you are painting a picture of this parable coming to life. What would be the center of your painting? Where will you put those on the first guest list? Who are they and how will you portray their legitimate excuses? And who are the outcasts in our society and world who would be on the second guest list? Where are they in your painting? Who is serving the banquet? Where would you put yourself? What are you doing? What are you feeling?

This parable teaches us something about the One who creates us and seeks relationship with all of God's children. God invites the guests (all humankind) to a banquet and promises to dine with them. The offer to share in the breaking of bread is a sign of God's blessing and promise of eternal fellowship. In the fellowship of the shared meal, all are bound together as God's people.

Jesus' parable also provides a biblical image of hospitality. We have been notified in advance of God's invitation. Our call is to join God's fellowship, and then we are to extend God's hospitality to others. Fred Craddock describes what we are to do: "Hospitality, then, is not having each other over on Friday evenings, but welcoming those who are in no position to host us in return."[4] God is a host we can never repay. God's invitation to eat together is a sign of God's saving grace through the blessing of relationship, and we are to offer that same grace to others.

Holy Communion

The creating God's continuing invitation to relationship and fellowship expressed in this parable is reenacted every time we participate in

Holy Communion. God's hospitality is extended to us when the invitation is given in the name of the One who redeems us:

> Christ our Lord invites to his table all who love him,
> who earnestly repent of their sin
> and seek to live in peace with one another.
> Therefore, let us confess our sin before God and one another.
> (*UMH*, p. 7)

A second form of the invitation is used in a traditional text from the Communion rituals of the former Methodist and former Evangelical United Brethren churches:

> Ye that do truly and earnestly repent of your sins,
> and are in love and charity with your neighbors,
> and intend to lead a new life, following the commandments of God,
> and walking from henceforth in his holy ways:
> Draw near with faith, and take this Holy Sacrament to your comfort,
> and make your humble confession to almighty God.
> (*UMH*, p. 26)

In Jesus Christ, God as Redeemer issues the first invitation to share the food of life. A second invitation to Christian fellowship is offered in our service of Holy Communion. Making a decision to accept this gift of grace we can never repay is a sacred moment. When we participate in Holy Communion, we participate as God's covenant people, the body of Christ. Paul wrote: "The cup of blessing that we bless, is it not a sharing in the blood of Christ? The bread that we break, is it not a sharing in the body of Christ? Because there is one bread, we who are many are one body, for we all partake of the one bread" (1 Cor. 10:16-17).

When we come to God's table, we agree to sit down in fellowship with our brothers and sisters, with all of God's children including those we often exclude. Paul reprimanded the Corinthians for their divisions and self-centeredness.

> When you come together, it is not really to eat the Lord's supper. For when the time comes to eat, each of you goes ahead with your own supper, and one goes hungry and another becomes drunk. What! Do you not have homes to eat and drink in? Or do you show contempt for the church of God and humiliate those who have nothing? (1 Cor. 11:20-22)

At God's table, we promise to set aside our own agendas to participate in the body of Christ. Then we are expected to go out and serve God's food of life to others. Charles Wesley expressed it well in this hymn:

> My message as from God receive;
> ye all may come to Christ and live.
> O let his love your hearts constrain,
> nor suffer him to die in vain.
>
> This is the time, no more delay!
> This is the Lord's accepted day.
> Come thou, this moment, at his call,
> and live for him who died for all.
> (*UMH* #339)

God's invitation to full participation in the body of Christ has been delivered. How will we respond?

Examine the rituals for Word and Table in the United Methodist Hymnal *for evidence of the themes of Jesus' parable in Luke. Can you find other ways in which our service of Holy Communion reveals the nature of God? Sing or read "Come, Sinners, to the Gospel Feast" (Charles Wesley;* UMH *#339) or "Here, O My Lord, I See Thee" (Horatius Bonar;* UMH *#623) for other interpretations of God's banquet.*

In this section, we have seen the creating God as a nurturing caregiver who loves us. The redeeming God, author of salvation, offers relationship to all of God's wayward children through this great love. We are invited to come to God's table as part of God's covenant people. Only through the work of God's sustaining Spirit within us will we be able to respond in faith.

The Way of Salvation

The creating God who invites us to the gospel feast is also the *redeeming God* who provides us with the means to attend the feast. This same God sustains us on our journey of faith. We experience the assurance of God's love as we see evidence of God's grace at work in our lives while others see fruits of our faith through the evidence of our daily living.

Vital Religious Experience

Through his own understanding of Scripture, tradition, and the evidence of his own religious experience, John Wesley recognized that faith is a pilgrimage, a process of growth. We have noted Wesley's early discussion with his mother about faith as a rational assent to certain beliefs. And we have seen Wesley at Aldersgate gaining a newfound trust in God as Savior, the One who redeems, coming to know the assurance of God's love.

As Wesley's faith journey progressed, his theology came to express his belief that we can "see" evidence of the redeeming God at work in our lives. (A more thorough examination of John Wesley's developing understanding of faith can be found in *LLDG,* chapter 6.) Vital religious experience has to do with the way we come to know God through the created order, through God's work in Jesus Christ, and through God's sustaining presence.

In other words, what Scripture teaches us about the nature of God is evident through our own religious experience.[5] We can know God's redeeming grace through the working of the Holy Spirit in us by changed lives.[6]

Stephen Gunter, author of *The Limits of Love Divine,* makes a case that Wesley's ministry did indeed focus on experience, God's work in the vital religious experience of salvation.

> Wesley's search for personal certainty of salvation led him to emphasize experiential religion to an extent that made many people uncomfortable, but it was experiential religion that had brought him spiritual peace. In Wesley's

> mind, to be extremely sensitive to the sentiments of those who opposed experiential religion would have meant that he was less sensitive to God's providential direction for Methodism. Among the Methodists experiential religion took precedence over ecclesiastical protocol and canon law.[7]

In this sense, Wesley's own religious experience shaped the Methodist renewal movement. Wesley was well versed in Scripture and in the historic tradition of the church and approached his ministry with the heart and mind of a reformer. But he focused on that which needed renewing in the Anglican tradition—the understanding of faith experience. Wesley's own struggle with an utterly rational faith occurred at a time when the church was highly rational as well. At Aldersgate, Wesley came to experience the assurance of God's grace through Jesus Christ. Theodore Runyon of Candler School of Theology concludes that "Aldersgate convinced Wesley that 'Christian experience' meant participating in an event of reconciliation that was initiated by God," the One who chooses us and blesses us.[8] Through the Methodist movement, Wesley called the church to know God with a "strangely warmed" heart.

So the source and criteria of experience in the Wesleyan quadrilateral means the vital religious experience of knowing God's reconciling love as revealed in Jesus Christ. When we talk about experience in this sense, we talk about how God has acted in history and is acting in our own lives through participation in Christian community. The fruits of this experience of faith are found in the way we live our lives. It becomes evident through our behavior that we walk the way of salvation *(via salutis)*.

Think about a significant event or time in your own life journey. What were the circumstances surrounding this experience? Who was present with you at the time? What happened to you as a result? Reflect on how God was at work through this time in your life. How do we know God's will at those turning points on the way of faith?

Via Salutis: *Invitation and Repentance*

God is the One who redeems us by offering the invitation to reconciliation and providing the way of salvation for those who will repent and come to God's table (*GOGK* addresses the way of salvation). But even repentance is impossible for us without God's help. "God's prevenient grace creates and prompts our spiritual desires, drawing us to faith in Jesus Christ."[9] *The creating God* who loves us and who has chosen to be in covenant with us provides the means for our repentance and salvation.

We can find a variety of images for the One who provides the way of salvation in our United Methodist documents. God is, first of all, a God of mercy who forgives us our sin:

> Depth of mercy! Can there be
> mercy still reserved for me?
> Can my God his wrath forbear,
> me, the chief of sinners, spare?
>
> Now incline me to repent,
> let me now my sins lament,
> now my foul revolt deplore,
> weep, believe, and sin no more.
> (Charles Wesley; *UMH* #355)

Charles Wesley provides us the image of a God whose mercy is great enough for even the worst of sinners. "Incline me to repent" refers to the work of God's prevenient grace, which woos us away from sin. A merciful God offers us a way out of our own self-destructive behavior before we ask.

Another perspective on the greatness of God's mercy can be found in the hymn "There's a Wideness in God's Mercy" (Frederick W. Faber; UMH *#121). Sing or read the words and notice the understanding of God that is portrayed in this hymn.*

Additional understanding of a redeeming God can be found in the definition of prevenient grace found in the *Book of Discipline:*

> We acknowledge God's prevenient grace, the divine love that surrounds all humanity and precedes any and all of our conscious impulses. This grace prompts our first wish to please God, our first glimmer of understanding concerning God's will, and our "first slight transient conviction" of having sinned against God.

> God's grace also awakens in us an earnest longing for deliverance from sin and death and moves us toward repentance and faith.
> (*BOD,* par. 65, p. 45)

Note the image here of the Creator God's love surrounding "all humanity." We know the breadth of God's redeeming love made manifest through the life, death, and resurrection of Jesus Christ. God's saving grace precedes our conscious response. God provides for our spiritual needs and gives us the courage to risk taking that first step toward a new relationship with God through Christ. Through God's love, we come to see the world and ourselves in a new way. We can see where we have fallen short and with God's help, we long to be faithful. The action words for God in this definition are "surrounds," "precedes," "prompts," "awakens," and "moves"—apt descriptors for God's redeeming work in Jesus Christ.

One section in the United Methodist Hymnal, *"The Power of the Holy Spirit," is organized around Wesley's understanding of* via salutis, *the way of salvation. Look at the hymns included in the section entitled "Prevenient Grace: Invitation and Repentance" (*UMH *#337-60). What can you learn about the One who is working in us, who invites us to repent and come to a new relationship through the gospel feast?*

Via Salutis: *Justifying Grace*

Once we have turned away from sin through repentance and set our eyes on God, we find *a redeeming God* who is willing to welcome a relationship with us. John Wesley believed we can know God's forgiveness through the assurance of God's saving love in Christ Jesus (justification). Justification means pardon, and God's justifying grace lifts the guilt of the past from us. The invitation to the gospel feast means we can begin life anew at God's table through our acceptance of a new relationship through God's grace.

The *Book of Discipline* describes God's justifying grace:

> We believe God reaches out to the repentant believer in justifying grace with accepting and pardoning love. Wesleyan theology stresses that a

> decisive change in the human heart can and does occur under the prompting of grace and the guidance of the Holy Spirit.
>
> In justification, we are, through faith, forgiven our sin and restored to God's favor. . . .
>
> This process of justification and new birth is often referred to as conversion. Such a change may be sudden and dramatic, or gradual and cumulative. It marks a new beginning, yet it is part of an ongoing process. (*BOD,* par. 65, p. 45)

We find images of God here as the One who reaches out, who prompts and guides us to change. For Wesley, the God of love and grace who offers us a new beginning through Jesus Christ is "God for us." With a change of heart, we are restored to God's favor, but we proceed under God's continuing guidance through the Holy Spirit. Again, Charles Wesley describes it with a hymn:

> What we have felt and seen,
> with confidence we tell,
> and publish to the ends of earth
> the signs infallible.
>
> We by his Spirit prove
> and know the things of God,
> the things which freely of his love
> he hath on us bestowed.
>
> (*UMH* #372)

For Wesley, the God whose sustaining presence is made known to us in the Holy Spirit is "God in us." God's redeeming work in our lives can be known through the One who sustains us. The word *know* is so important to Wesley because it reveals much about his understanding of the nature of God. God is not aloof and inaccessible to us. Although there is much about God that is a mystery, we can know God's saving grace in our lives. We can know we are in relationship with God, and our experience of knowing is called *assurance*. In Charles Wesley's words, assurance is a moment of awakening:

> Long my imprisoned spirit lay,
> fast bound in sin and nature's night;
> thine eye diffused a quickening ray;
> I woke, the dungeon flamed with light;
> my chains fell off, my heart was free,
> I rose, went forth, and followed thee.
> (*UMH* #363)

Review the section "Justifying Grace" in the United Methodist Hymnal *(#361-81). What images of God do you find?*

Via Salutis: *Sanctifying Grace*

God does not finish with us at our rebirth. Like a loving parent, God tends our growth. God's prevenient grace and justifying grace draw us toward lives that are increasingly in tune with God's will for us. This process is known as sanctification, growing toward Christian perfection.

A description of God's continuing work of sanctification in us can also be found in the *Book of Discipline:*

> We hold that the wonder of God's acceptance and pardon does not end God's saving work, which continues to nurture our growth in grace. Through the power of the Holy Spirit we are enabled to increase in the knowledge and love of God and in love for our neighbor.
>
> New birth is the first step in this process of sanctification. Sanctifying grace draws us toward the gift of Christian perfection, which Wesley described as a heart "habitually filled with the love of God and neighbor" and as "having the mind of Christ and walking as he walked."
>
> This gracious gift of God's power and love, the hope and expectation of the faithful, is neither warranted by our efforts nor limited by our frailties. (*BOD,* par. 65, p. 46)

Here we see *a sustaining God* whose saving work continues. God's gift of salvation is unearned and free. God is a God of power and love who passes on that power and love to us through rebirth. God's love knows no bounds, and through us God's love is extended through our relationship with others. Charles Wesley's great hymn describes God's marvelous love:

> Love divine, all loves excelling,
> joy of heaven, to earth come down;
> Fix in us thy humble dwelling;
> all thy faithful mercies crown!
> Jesus, thou art all compassion,
> pure, unbounded love thou art;
> visit us with thy salvation;
> enter every trembling heart.
>
> Finish, then, thy new creation;
> pure and spotless let us be.
> Let us see thy great salvation
> perfectly restored in thee;
> changed from glory into glory,
> till in heaven we take our place,
> till we cast our crowns before thee,
> lost in wonder, love, and praise.
>
> (*UMH* #384)

This hymn reflects the theme that God's love is greater than any other love we have known. Our God is a God of joy who lives in us. We have been assured that God is faithful in this relationship, full of compassion, and pure. God is the source of our salvation and merits our wonder, love, and praise.

*Examine hymns under "Rebirth and the New Creature" (*UMH *#382-94, the section "Sanctifying and Perfecting Grace") for additional images of God.*

Our Response in Faith

We have been thinking together about who God is and what God has done and is doing. God is our Creator, the One beyond us, who invites us to fellowship under God's rule, and God's prevenient or preceding grace gives us the inclination to accept this invitation. We also know *God as Redeemer,* the One among us, who provides a way of salvation through the witness of the life, death, and resurrection of Jesus Christ. God's justifying grace brings us assurance of our pardon and salvation when we repent and come to a new relationship with God through Jesus Christ. And God's sanctifying grace through the Holy Spirit perfects us for Christ-like living.

Now we turn our attention to the question of what God expects of us. *God as Sustainer,* the One within us, is at work in the daily lives of God's people. Jesus Christ is a model for how we are to live, and he taught us what God expects of us under God's rule. God's continuing and perfecting work within us is seen in the evidence of a life of holiness. In John Wesley's words: "When we, by grace, appropriate faith to believe that Christ is our savior, then the reality of Christ's righteousness becomes an experiential reality in our lives. We receive certainty of this by witness of the Spirit."[10] We have evidence in our lives of the indwelling Christ as we live in love of God and neighbor.

When we experience God's justifying grace, it is a day of new beginnings. Remember days of new beginnings in your faith journey. Then celebrate God's work for us and in us by singing or reading "This Is a Day of New Beginnings" (Brian Wren; UMH *#383).*

A righteous life is a life of holiness. Samuel and Susanna Wesley both influenced John Wesley's understanding of holiness. For the Wesleys, the foundation for a life of holiness was trust in the providence of God. Letters to John from the Wesleys reflect their steady dependence on the providence of God. Samuel wrote: "I've done what I could; do you the same, and rest the whole with Providence."[11] What is meant by God's providence is "that all things, all events in this world, are under the management of God."[12] In his sermon "On Divine Providence," John Wesley states:

> If you truly fear God, you need fear none beside. [God] will be a strong tower to all that trust in [God], from the face of your enemies. What is there either in heaven or in earth that can harm you while you are under the care of the Creator and Governor of heaven and earth? Let all earth

> and all hell combine against you—yea, the whole animate and inanimate creation—they cannot harm while God is on your side; [God's] favourable kindness covers you "as a shield."[13]

For the Wesleys, the foundation of holiness was trust in the God who loves the whole of creation. And their guiding principle for a life of holiness was love to God and love to neighbor, "the principle and rule of all our thoughts, words, and actions, with respect to either."[14]

Take some time to examine the "Providence" section of the United Methodist Hymnal *(#126-43) to see how providence is understood by the hymn writers.*

*Charles Wesley wrote "I Want a Principle Within" (*UMH *#410) to express the guiding principle of the Wesleys' life. Read the words of this hymn and consider the understanding of God it portrays. What kind of God makes us want a principle within? How is God's role portrayed in this hymn?*

God does not create us and then abandon us. On our pilgrimage of faith, God shows us the way and gives us our work to do. In response to God's love for us, we are to do everything to the glory of God. John Wesley wrote: "I entirely agree that 'the glory of God, and the different degrees of promoting it, are to be our sole consideration and direction in the choice of any course of life.' "[15] This principle provides a means for discerning God's will and direction. It is the measure of a holy life.

Practical Divinity

What God expects of us is the practice of faith, the work God gives us to do. The Wesleys called this work "practical divinity." Susanna Wesley first described her understanding of practical divinity in a letter to her daughter, Sukey. Learning things by heart or saying prayers is not enough, she wrote. "You must understand what you say, and you must practice what you know."[16] Susanna Wesley believed we need knowledge requisite to the practice of faith. And the rule for the practice of faith (practical divinity) was love to God and love to neighbor. In his sermon "Marks of the New Birth," John Wesley described this response to God's love:

> The necessary fruit of this love of God is the love of our neighbour, of every soul which God hath made; not excepting our enemies, not excepting those who are now "despitefully using and persecuting us"; a love whereby we love every [human] *as ourselves*—as we love our own souls. Nay, our Lord has expressed it still more strongly, teaching us to "love one another even as [God] hath loved us."[17]

In this passage, Wesley reflects his understanding of a God who is Creator of us all and expects us to love creation in the same way.

For Wesley, practical divinity includes inner piety and social holiness:

> And while he thus always exercises his love to God, by prayer without ceasing, rejoicing evermore, and in everything giving thanks, this commandment is written in his heart, that "he who loveth God, loves his brother [and sister] also." And he accordingly "loves his neighbour as himself"; he loves every [human] as his own soul.[18]

Inner piety is responding to God at work in us. The development of our personal relationship with God is expressed through "praying without ceasing, rejoicing evermore, and in everything giving thanks."

Social holiness is loving our neighbor with our whole heart. John Wesley understood that God is calling our faith community to action through social holiness:

> Here are poor families to be relieved; here are children to be educated; here are workhouses wherein both young and old want and gladly receive the word of exhortation; here are prisons to be visited, wherein alone is a complication of all human wants; and lastly, here are the schools of the prophets, here are tender minds to be formed and strengthened, and babes in Christ to be instructed and perfected in all useful learning.[19]

Social holiness or love to neighbor is a response to God's love already at work in us. In the sermon "On Working Out Our Own Salvation," John Wesley emphasizes "that God initiates [Father], God enables [Son], God continually empowers the believer [Holy Spirit], and God receives the glory."[20] We can do nothing on our own. All the good we are able to do is accomplished because God created us, provides us the way of salvation, and is working in us and through us.

A hymn that expresses some of the need in our world is "Where Cross the Crowded Ways of Life" (Frank Mason North; UMH *#427). What is the understanding of God expressed in this hymn? How do we know what God expects of us? What are the images or metaphors for Jesus Christ, the One who redeems us?*

We believe God invites us to repent and to accept God's justifying grace. As God's people, we know we are able to respond in faith and obedience to God's call through the Holy Spirit working in us. We learned in our study of the Beatitudes that God shows us what is expected under God's rule. And the Wesleys' principle for living under God's rule is love to God and love to neighbor, the practice of faith through personal and social holiness.

Faith Worked by Love

Since New Testament times, the church has reflected on what God expects of us. Across time, Christians have asked, How is God's work in salvation related to personal and social holiness, to faith and good works? Wesley learned that salvation by faith is more than rational assent alone and more than an emotional response alone. God expects us to participate in the righteousness of Jesus Christ through our practice of faith.

Our doctrinal standards in the "Articles of Religion" and the "Confession of Faith" state the United Methodist understanding of what God expects of us through faith and good works.

Article X.—Of Good Works

> Although good works, which are the fruits of faith, and follow after justification, cannot put away our sins, and endure the severity of God's judgment; yet are they pleasing and acceptable to God in Christ, and spring out of a true and lively faith, insomuch that by them a lively faith may be as evidently known as a tree is discerned by its fruit. (*BOD*, par. 67, p. 61)

Article X.—Good Works

> We believe good works are the necessary fruits of faith and follow regeneration but they do not have the virtue to remove our sins or to avert divine judgment. We believe good works, pleasing and acceptable to God in Christ, spring from a true and living faith, for through and by them faith is made evident. (*BOD,* par. 67, p. 68)

We learn from these statements that God is pleased by our good works as evidence of our faith. But good works alone cannot atone for our sinfulness. A gracious God who invites us into relationship is our only source of forgiveness. Good works are the result of our justification by God's saving grace. Wesley emphasized God's continuing work for us and in us: "The condition for initial salvation is *faith.* The condition for continued salvation is *faith.* The condition for final salvation is *faith.* . . . it was a living experiential reality; therefore, true saving faith 'worked by love.' "[21] God works for us and in us on our behalf, and God expects we will be righteous toward others.

The United Methodist understanding of "saving faith worked by love" finds expression in the "Social Principles," a call to corporate dialogue about our practice of faith as a people (*BOD,* par. 70-75, pp. 87-106). The preamble states our understanding of who God is, what God is doing on our behalf, and what God expects of us:

> We, the people called United Methodists, affirm our faith in God our Creator and Father, in Jesus Christ our Savior, and in the Holy Spirit, our Guide and Guard.
>
> We acknowledge our complete dependence upon God in birth, in life, in death, and in life eternal. Secure in God's love, we affirm the goodness of life and confess our many sins against God's will for us as we find it in Jesus Christ. We have not always been faithful stewards of all that has been committed to us by God the Creator. We have been reluctant followers of Jesus Christ in his mission to bring all persons into a community of love. Though called by the Holy Spirit to become new creatures in Christ, we have resisted the further call to become the people of God in our dealings with each other and the earth on which we live.
>
> Grateful for God's forgiving love, in which we live and by which we

> are judged, and affirming our belief in the inestimable worth of each individual, we renew our commitment to become faithful witnesses to the gospel, not alone to the ends of earth, but also to the depths of our common life and work. (*BOD*, pp. 87-88)

The "Social Principles" begin with an affirmation of a God who is made known in different ways through the Trinity. The second paragraph is an illumination of the first and describes in more detail what God as Creator, Redeemer, and Sustainer has done for us. We are reminded of our failure to live a holy life. As a church, we are called to a new commitment as faithful witnesses of the gospel. Three short paragraphs reflect our entire tradition about who God is, what God has done, what God is doing, and what God expects of us!

CHAPTER FIVE

The God We Worship

THROUGHOUT OUR STUDY, WE HAVE JOURNEYED TOGETHER IN FAITH, SECURE IN OUR BELIEF THAT GOD IS WITH US AS WE LEARN. We have reflected together about who God is and what God has done. We began our study with Jacob and have followed his footsteps through a story of human sinfulness, wrestling, blessing and covenant, and finally obedience. Jacob's story is the story of God's people, our story. For we, too, wrestle with ourselves and with God over our sinfulness. And then, we discover once again a merciful and loving God waiting patiently for us to repent and accept God's saving grace. In gratitude and love to God, we seek to be obedient to God's will in our lives by loving our neighbor. To be reconciled with God and our neighbor is to be home. Charles Wesley reflects the joy and peace of being at home in God in the final verse of "Wrestling Jacob":

> Lame as I am, I take the prey,
> hell, earth, and sin with ease overcome;
> I leap for joy, pursue my way,
> and as a bounding hart fly home,
> through all eternity to prove
> thy nature, and thy name is Love.
>
> (*UMH* #387)

In this final chapter, we turn to the issue of how we talk about God and the many ways we celebrate and affirm the greatness of the God we worship. To be one with God and our neighbor means we recognize the richness that diversity of cultural heritage and language brings to our life together.

As we have studied together, we have looked for images and names of God that are part of our heritage as United Methodists and part of our individual religious experience. Some of us may have been stretched as we have expanded our awareness and our vocabularies in order to talk about who God is and what God has done in new ways. J. B. Phillips once wrote:

> The trouble with many people today is that they have not found a God big enough for modern needs. While their experience of life has grown in a score of directions, and their mental horizons have been expanded to the point of bewilderment by world events and by scientific discoveries, their ideas of God have remained largely static.[1]

Phillips reminds us that the God we worship is greater than all of life. With the Wesleys, we affirm our trust in the One who cares for all of creation.

Faith Seeking Expression

For us to name God implies that we know who God is, and we do know much about the nature of God. Yet we recognize that God is always greater than what we know or the names we give.

> How can we name a Love that wakens heart and mind,
> indwelling all we know or think or do or seek or find?
> Within our daily world, in every human face,
> Love's echoes sound and God is found, hid in the commonplace.
>
> So in a hundred names, each day we all can meet
> a presence, sensed and shown at work, at home, or in the street.
> Yet every name we see, shines in a brighter sun:
> In Christ alone is Love full grown and life and hope begun.
>
> (Brian Wren, *UMH* #111)[2]

The names we use for God reflect what we believe about the nature of God. To limit the way we talk about God narrows our understanding of God. Expanding the way we talk about God brings a growth in our understanding of God. Language and thinking are closely interrelated. In *Words That Hurt, Words That Heal: Language About God and People,* we read:

> The language we use about God reflects and shapes how we think about God.
>
> Language both accentuates and limits our ability to communicate God's power and love. Words, being of human origin, are both liberating and restricting. We need to search for more creative ways of expressing our relationship to God. The search is ongoing and continually needs to be sensitive to all segments of society. (*WTH,* 3)

The way we talk about who God is, what God has done, what God is doing, and what God expects of us takes on a new dimension in an increasingly diverse and complex culture. All around us we can see concern for faith seeking expression that is meaningful for our time. For example, the committee that worked on the New Revised Standard Version of the Bible affirmed the importance of the message of the Bible for all those who seek to hear what God is saying to them:

> That message must not be disguised in phrases that are no longer clear, or hidden under words that have changed or lost their meaning; it must be presented in language that is direct and plain and meaningful to people today.[3]

In other words, the message of the Bible cannot be diminished by sharing it in meaningful ways. John Wesley's principle of "plain truth for plain people" means sharing the gospel with others in language they can understand.

The challenge for us is to find ways to celebrate the contributions to our understanding of God from those who differ from us in gender, race, ethnicity, or culture. Some of us are excited about the possibilities of using varied imagery and more inclusive language for the God we worship while others are uncomfortable with these different expressions of who God is and what God has done. Some want to maintain our traditional ways of talking about God. But as the authors of *Language of Hospitality* point out,

> We will not reach full humanity as women and men as long as our language and images continue to limit us, often in unconscious ways. A five-year-old playing with friends argued that boys are better than girls. When they asked why, he responded, "Because God is a boy, isn't he?"[4]

When we use God language that consistently excludes women or other persons who are different from ourselves, we are limiting God. Our static ideas about who God is and what God has done shut us off from our neighbors.

On the other hand, when we use varied imagery and language to express our faith in God, we are continuing the practice of others who interpreted their belief in God in new ways for their time. We have learned that the nature of God is revealed in *Scripture* in a variety of ways. The Hebrew people believed God's name was so holy that it should never be said aloud. This is the God of Jacob, the God whose name was withheld when Jacob wrestled with the unknown traveler throughout the night. The people of Israel called God "YAHWEH," "I AM WHO I AM" (Exod. 3:13-15). YAHWEH is LORD, the One who acts in history in relationship to God's covenant people. In the New Testament, a variety of images for God are used, but we also find an emerging pattern of naming God as Father, Son, and Holy Spirit.

The *tradition* of our church also has given us additional ways to talk about a God who is made known to us in different ways as the Trinity: the One beyond us who created all that is, the One among us in Jesus Christ, and the One within us as sustaining presence.

And we have come to know God through our own religious *experience*. The conflict over language as expression of faith comes mainly out of our different faith experiences, which have been influenced by our gender and the environments in which we have lived. Our experience shapes our expression of faith. We often notice language differences in accent and meanings of words or phrases as we travel from one part of our country to another. The differences may become even more pronounced when we visit other countries in various parts of the world. In each of these places, the meaning of faith experience is expressed in ways that are best understood in that faith community.

The issue at stake in the discussion about the language of faith is the right of each person and faith community to contribute to our understanding of God through their own expressions of faith. Because God is greater than all of us and made known to us in many ways, the varied expressions of faith add a richness to our understanding of God.

*Examine hymns from various cultures in the "God's Nature" section of the hymnal (*UMH *#107, #110, #116, #119, #120). Look at the imagery and phrases used to describe God. What images seem particularly striking to you and enrich your understanding of God?*

In keeping with a commitment to communicate our faith in God in ways that are inclusive of a diverse membership and understandable for our time, the 1988 General Conference of The United Methodist Church established language guidelines for the new *Book of Worship:*

1. All texts shall be tested by the Wesleyan quadrilateral of Scripture, tradition, experience, and reason.
2. All texts shall be examined to determine what they state or imply in regard to:
   a. care of God's creation;
   b. human rights, with respect for all races and cultures and both sexes, and with equal opportunity and dignity for all persons;
   c. international understanding and cooperation;
   d. the eradication of war and the establishment of peace.
3. Avoid language that discriminates against women, against any racial or ethnic community, or against persons with handicapping conditions.
4. Seek a balanced diversity of scriptural imagery in addressing or referring to God. (*BOW,* 1992 Daily Christian Advocate, Advance Edition, vol. 3, R-39)

Examine one of the "General Services" in the Book of Worship *to see how these guidelines are reflected in the language of the service. How does language reflect and shape our understanding of God?*

As United Methodists, we celebrate the diversity of peoples who are part of our church, knowing we are united as God's children. "As Christians, we believe that we are children of God, created in God's image, and members of the family of God; we believe that diversity is a gift of the creative genius of God and that languages are an expression of the wisdom of God" (*BOR,* p. 163).

This gift of diversity can be experienced when we join in worship with brothers and sisters from differing cultural heritages. To sing and pray and listen to the gospel in languages other than our own begins to push our imaginations to encompass God's greatness.

Unity in Diversity

Even though we are a diverse people, we are one in the body of Christ and part of God's household. This excerpt from *Language of Hospitality* explains it well:

> The household of God is a multiethnic, multicultural and multilingual family. It is comprised of a rainbow of people and we are part of it. In the household of God, our ethnic/cultural/linguistic heritage, which includes our color, are our gifts to one another. We bring them with us into life in God's household. They are gifts. We are to value them in ourselves and in others. The Christian gives particular expression to the household of God by relating to others within the household in Christlike ways.[5]

As we read this statement, we are reminded once again of the gospel feast and God's invitation to relationship with God and with one another. Through God's gracious invitation to share the bread of life, we are called to extend God's hospitality to others, regardless of race, gender, class, age, or handicapping conditions. We are to treat others as God through Christ has treated us. "Hospitality refers to reflecting in our language and behavior toward others a friendly, receptive, and welcoming love. . . . It is the acknowledgement in our heart, our behavior, and our language that we are all kinsfolk in Jesus Christ."[6]

Not only are we to extend hospitality to sisters and brothers of the faith, but we are to relate to all peoples as neighbor. In "Called to Be Neighbors and Witnesses," our church gives form to what it means to be a neighbor, to extend God's hospitality to others:

> It means to meet other persons, to know them, to relate to them, to respect them, and to learn about their ways which may be quite different from our own. It means to create a sense of community in our neighborhoods, towns, and cities, and to make them places in which the unique customs of each group of people can be expressed and their values protected. It means to create social structures in which there is justice for all and in which everyone can participate in shaping their life together "in community." Each race or group of people is not only allowed to be who they are, but their way of life is valued and given full expression. (*BOR*, p. 264)

This statement portrays an expectation about our actions toward others in response to what God is doing for us.

One response to what God has done and is doing for us has taken form through the "Social Principles" of The United Methodist Church. The Social Principles are "intended to be instructive and persuasive in the best of the prophetic spirit. The Social Principles are a call to all members of The United Methodist Church to a prayerful, studied dialogue of faith and practice" (*BOR*, p. 31). The Social Principles call God's people to social holiness.

Since 1968, each General Conference of The United Methodist Church has considered numerous resolutions that turn the Social Principles into action. *The Book of Resolutions* is an elaboration of each section of the "Social Principles" and is a source for serious dialogue about how God is calling us to live. The resolutions interpret what God wants us to do in our time in light of Scripture, tradition, experience, and reason. During each General Conference, some resolutions are retained, some are amended, and others are deleted or added. The resolutions are a means for the church to extend God's love, mercy, and justice to others in contemporary situations.

> The Social Principles [*BOD*, par. 70-76] provide our most recent official summary of stated convictions that seek to apply the Christian vision of righteousness to social, economic, and political issues. Our historic opposition to evils such as smuggling, inhumane prison conditions, slavery, drunkenness, and child labor was founded upon a vivid sense of God's wrath against human injustice and wastage.
>
> Our struggles for human dignity and social reform have been a response to God's demand for love, mercy, and justice in the light of the Kingdom. We proclaim no *personal gospel* that fails to express itself in relevant social concerns; we proclaim no *social gospel* that does not include the personal transformation of sinners.
>
> It is our conviction that the good news of the Kingdom must judge, redeem, and reform the sinful social structures of our time. (*BOD*, par. 65, p. 48)

Here we see what God expects of us stated in terms of a life of righteousness, a life of personal and social holiness. God's saving grace is available not only for setting our lives right, but for setting society right as well.

One example of the call to action through love to God and love to neighbor is the resolution on "Advocacy for the Poor":

> Whereas, the pastoral letter from the Council of Bishops, November 14, 1982, said: "As Christians we acknowledge that implicit in the faith of the church is a mandate for action. It is not enough to experience deep distress over the plight of the hungry and hopeless victims of the economic crisis." The gospel demands that we manifest our love for Christ through our efforts to relieve the suffering of those who are without food and shelter, who live under the burden of the current economic catastrophe and increasing social injustices. (1988 *BOR*, p. 328)

In this resolution, we can see the reflection of our heritage of personal piety and social holiness, of the interconnectedness of faith and good works. What God has done for us in Christ demands that we share love with those who are suffering the effects of poverty. God's people in The United Methodist Church are called on specifically "to be an advocate for the poor and oppressed people of all nations, acting with a sense of justice, compassion, understanding, and God's presence" (1988 *BOR*, p. 328). Congregations are called on to effect change in public policy toward greater economic justice (1988 *BOR*, p. 329).

*From the section "The Social Community," select a resolution that addresses an issue of ethnic or racial diversity (*BOR*, pp. 151, 162, 164, 178, 190, 191, 193, 196, 206, 209, 210, 247, 248, 254, 256, 263, 285, 303, 306, 320, 321, 322, 324, 338, 339, 340, 345, 346, 349, 364, 366, 376, 383). Read the resolution and consider what the resolution states or assumes about who God is, what God is doing, and what God expects of us.*

Through God's covenant with us and God's Spirit at work in us, life is different for those who accept the invitation to God's table. Through our new relationship with God, United Methodists are called to live by the principle of love to God and love to neighbor. The fruits of God's Spirit at work in us become evident in our relationships with one another and with God as we continue life in a complex and complicated world. In the midst of our diversity, we stand in unity as the body of Christ, as God's people.

> United Methodists as a diverse people continue to strive for consensus in understanding the gospel. In our diversity, we are held together by a shared inheritance and a common desire to participate in the creative and redemptive activity of God.
>
> Our task is to articulate our vision in a way that will draw us together as a people in mission. (*BOD*, par. 68, p. 83)

As United Methodists, our challenge is to come to know one another better as we celebrate the God we worship. Through sharing in the unique gifts of our sisters and brothers, we can gain new insights into who God is, what God has done, what God is doing, and what God expects of us. We become interpreters of the Good News for one another.

Thy Nature and Thy Name Is Love

As we come to the end of this study, we celebrate our growth in faith and our new understandings of who God is, what God has done, what

God is doing, and what God expects of us. In our study, we have affirmed these beliefs about God:

—God is the God of all creation, the One who chooses to be in relationship with God's people.
—God relates to God's people through blessing and covenant, and God is always faithful in this relationship.
—God is known to us in different ways as the One who creates us (Creator), the One who redeems us (Christ), and the One who sustains us (Holy Ghost).
—God invites us into new relationship and provides the way of salvation for us.
—God patiently awaits our response in faith for all that God has done and is doing for us.
—God expects that we will share God's hospitality with others.
—God is known to us in many ways through many names and faces.

APPENDIXES

1
Study Session Guide

Note: For all sessions, use material in *italic* print for one-to-one, small group, or whole group discussions. Chapters 2 through 4 may be covered in three sessions as outlined here for more in-depth study or modified for one study session.

CHAPTER 1

Session 1: Preparation for the Journey (pp. 19-27)

Resources Needed: Bibles, *United Methodist Hymnals.*

Preparation: Read Introduction and chapter 1 of *The God We Worship.*

Suggestions:

• Offer some ways for class members to creatively express their relationships with God (write, draw, symbolize, mime, dance, model clay).

• Have each class member share with one other person about how God has been at work in some significant events that have shaped that person's life.

• Begin to compile a class list of names and images for God by recording all your suggestions on newsprint. Post the newsprint so that you can add other names and images for God to your class list as you discover them.

• Close with a time of reflection by sharing any insights or questions that have come to you during this session. Then sing or read aloud two verses of Charles Wesley's hymn "Come, O Thou Traveler Unknown" as a benediction.

CHAPTER 2

Session 2: A Tale of Deceit and Blessing (pp. 29-34)

Resources Needed: Bibles, *United Methodist Hymnals.*

Preparation: Read the story of Jacob in Genesis 27:1-45; 28:10-22; and 32:1–33:17.

Suggestions:

• Examine Genesis 32:22-32 for images and names for God. Add these names and images to your class list.

• Close your session by reading Psalm 23 or 46. Listen for the images of God portrayed by the psalmist.

Session 3: Salvation by Faith (pp. 34-40)

Resources Needed: Bibles, *United Methodist Hymnals, Book of Discipline.*

Preparation: Read Ephesians 2:8 and write a short paragraph about what it means for you. Read pages 9-11 and paragraph 67, pages 71-73 in *The Book of Discipline.*

Suggestions:

• Find some creative ways to describe how God's grace has been active in your life: Write a poem, tell a story, paint a picture, create a dance. If you wish, share something of the power of your discovery of God's grace with a friend.

• Add any new images or names for God to your class list.

• Close the session by singing or reading the words to hymn #606. In one word, take turns naming an image of God that is meaningful to you. Then close with a prayer or benediction.

Session 4: God's Blessing, Our Invitation (pp. 41-48)

Resources Needed: Bibles, *United Methodist Hymnals,* Bible dictionary and commentaries, *Book of Discipline.*

Preparation: Read Matthew 5:1-11.

Suggestions:

• Use magazines, newsprint, scissors, and glue to create a montage of pictures to illustrate your understanding of the nature of God as reflected in the promise of one of the Beatitudes.

• Covenant with your group to live out some part of a Beatitude for the next week.

• End the session by sharing your answers to our questions: Who is God? What has God done? Then sing or read Charles Wesley's hymn "Christ, from Whom All Blessings Flow" (*UMH* #550). Close with the "Prayer for a New Heart" (*UMH* #392).

CHAPTER 3

Session 5: The Creeds: Early Statements of Faith (pp. 49-57)

Resources Needed: Bibles, *United Methodist Hymnals, Book of Discipline,* Bible dictionary and commentaries.

Preparation: Read "Our Doctrinal Heritage" in the *Book of Discipline* (par. 65, pp. 40-48). What understanding of God is part of "Our Common Heritage as Christians"? What is distinctively Wesleyan about our belief?

Suggestions:

• Think about how your family or church tradition has shaped your relationship to the Trinity. The most common form of address in your personal prayers and in your church prayers—God, Jesus, Spirit—may be an indicator of the tradition that shaped you and your faith community. After time for reflection, share what you have discovered with at least one other person in your study group.

• Divide the following passages in the Gospel of John among your group members for study to see what each passage has to say about the relationship between God, Jesus, and Spirit: 1:1-18, 1:32-34, 5:19-24, 5:31-38, 10:11-18, 12:44-50, 14:1-7, 14:25-31, 15:26-27, 16:13-15. What dimensions of the Trinity are not discussed? Add any new images of God to your class list.

• Use your Bible commentaries and dictionary to look up biblical references for God, Jesus Christ, Spirit, Holy Spirit, and Trinity. You may want to assign one of these words to two or three persons to research together. Share what you learn about the Trinity with the group.

• As you close the session, invite each person to share a phrase or one sentence affirmation of faith about what she or he believes. Sing or read "Creating God, Your Fingers Trace" (Jeffery Rowthorn; *UMH* #109), and close with the "Trinity Sunday" prayer (*UMH* #76).

Session 6: The Doctrinal Standards of The United Methodist Church (pp. 57-62)

Resources Needed: Bibles, *United Methodist Hymnals, Book of Discipline, Book of Worship.*

Preparation: Read the historical documents of The United Methodist Church in the *Book of Discipline:* "Historical Statement," pages 9-20; "Articles of Religion," paragraph 67, pages 58-65; the "Confession of Faith," paragraph 67, pages 65-70.

Suggestions:

• As a class, talk about the ways in which history shapes identity.

• Close your session by reading together the litany for Heritage Sunday (*BOW* #426), remembering God's people who have contributed to our heritage of faith. Then share your statement of faith and sing or read "O Love, How Deep" (*UMH* #267).

Session 7: An Ecumenical Covenant (pp. 63-67)

Resources Needed: Bibles, *United Methodist Hymnals, Book of Discipline, COCU Consensus.*

Preparation: Read "Our Common Heritage as Christians" and "Basic Christian Affirmations" (*BOD,* par. 65, pp. 40-43). Ask a friend from another denomination to share a basic doctrinal standard or statement about the Trinity from his or her tradition and bring it with you to class.

Suggestions:

• If you have access to a copy of the *COCU Consensus* (check with your pastor or conference office), pick one of the sections on faith, worship, or ministry and see how the Trinitarian formula is used in the theological statement for that section. Look at the descriptive words and phrases to see how the relationship between God, Christ, and Spirit is portrayed. What images of God can you find stated or assumed?

• Allow time at the end of the session to share connections between the doctrinal standards or statements of other denominations and the creeds, the foundational documents of The United Methodist Church, or the *COCU Consensus.*

• To close your time together, sing or read "O God in Heaven" (Elena G. Maquiso; *UMH* #119) and share the "Canticle of Covenant Faithfulness" (Isa. 55:6-11; see *UMH* #125).

CHAPTER 4

Session 8: God's Invitation (pp. 69-74)

Resources Needed: Bibles, *United Methodist Hymnals.*

Preparation: Read Luke 14:16-23 and think about God's invitation to us. Based on this passage, write your own invitation to the gospel feast. Based on this passage, how would you describe the One who invites us?

Suggestions:

• Begin your study by sharing insights you have gained from your study thus far. What have you learned about who God is and what God has done?

• Take some time to share your thoughts about how your class contributes to your individual faith journey. How do faith journeys of class members affect the life of your group? What happens in the interaction?

• What have been your images of God as you participate in Communion services? Share feelings about how God works through Holy Communion in small groups.

• To close the session, sing or read Charles Wesley's hymn, "Come, Sinners, to the Gospel Feast" (*UMH* #339).

Session 9: The Way of Salvation (pp. 74-81)

Resources Needed: Bibles, *United Methodist Hymnals.*

Preparation: Read "Our Distinctive Heritage as United Methodists" (*BOD,* par. 65, pp. 44-47). Then select a favorite hymn from the "Justifying Grace" section of the *United Methodist Hymnal* (#361-

81) and list the characteristics or qualities of God you find reflected in the words.

Suggestions:

• Select one hymn you know well and one that is new to you from the section "Justifying Grace" in the *United Methodist Hymnal* (#361-81). With two other persons in your group, read the hymn and note what you can learn about the nature of God from the hymn. Share what you find with the rest of the class.

• Spend some time singing your favorite hymns from the sections of the hymnal we have studied in this session.

• Close the session by reading or singing "This Is a Day of New Beginnings" (Brian Wren; *UMH* #383). Offer a prayer of thanksgiving for God's saving grace at work in us.

Session 10: Our Response in Faith (pp. 81-87)

Resources Needed: *United Methodist Hymnals, Book of Discipline.*

Preparation: Read the "Social Principles" of The United Methodist Church (*BOD*, par. 70-75, pp. 87-106).

Suggestions:

• Divide your class into two groups. Have one explore hymns under "Personal Holiness" (*UMH* #395-424) and the other review hymns under "Social Holiness" (*UMH* #425-50). As you consider these hymns and prayers, think about how they express what God expects of us. Share any new insights with the class.

• Assign sections of "The Social Principles" (*BOD*, par. 70-75, pp. 87-106) to groups of two or three persons. Examine how the understanding of God we see in the Preamble is stated or implied. Is there a particular emphasis on one person of the Trinity: God as made known through creation, through Jesus Christ, or through the sustaining presence of the Holy Spirit? Note the church's interpretation of what God expects us to do. Share any insights you find with the class.

• To close the session, read "Our Social Creed" (*BOD*, par. 76, pp. 106-7) together. Then sing or read "Forth in Thy Name, O Lord" (Charles Wesley; *UMH* #438), and end with a prayer, "For Holiness of Heart" (*UMH* #401).

CHAPTER 5

Session 11: The God We Worship (pp. 89-98)

Resources Needed: *United Methodist Hymnals, Book of Worship, Book of Resolutions.*

Preparation: Compile a list of all the names and images for God you have used in our study together.

Suggestions:

• Review all the names and images for God you have collected and compile a list of your favorite names for God, including any new images or names you have discovered in this study. Write the names on brightly colored pieces of paper and post them on all sides of your room to symbolize the greatness of God's love.

• Read the additional guidelines about language (*BOW*, 1992 Daily Christian Advocate, Advance Edition, vol. 3, R38-40) and discuss.

• If you have participated in cross-cultural worship services in which several languages were spoken, share something of your experience with your class.

• Celebrate the diversity of our United Methodist Church and the greatness of the God we worship by reading "Praising God of Many Names" (*UMH* #104). Then sing "God of Many Names" (Brian Wren; *UMH* #105). Pause between each verse of the hymn to read your favorite names for God you have posted around the room. Offer a prayer of thanksgiving for the One who is made known to us in different ways.

• To celebrate the diversity among us, take some time to share experiences from your own cultural heritage or from opportunities to be a part of other cultures. How do these cross-cultural experiences shape our understanding of who God is and what God has done? Sing "Many Gifts, One Spirit" (Al Carmines; *UMH* #114) as a prayer hymn.

• Add your own affirmations to this list and create a celebration of our God whose name is love. Sing "Help Us Accept Each Other" (Fred Kaan; *UMH* #560). Join together in renewing your commitment to the God we worship by sharing in "Wesley's Covenant Service" (*BOW*, p. 291). Read your affirmations about who God is and what God has done. Then sing "God of Many Names" (Brian Wren; *UMH* #105) and close with "A Covenant Prayer in the Wesleyan Tradition" (*UMH* #607).

FOR FURTHER STUDY AND ACTION: Read the "Program to Emphasize Inclusiveness in All Dimensions of the Church" (*BOR*, pp. 346-48) and make further plans for study of inclusiveness in The United Methodist Church. Plan for specific actions that will increase your congregation's awareness of the gifts that diversity brings to our worship of the One who created us, the One who redeemed us through Jesus Christ, and the One who sustains our lives through the presence of the Holy Spirit.

2
Annotated Bibliography and Keys to Citations and References

Abraham, William J., "The Wesleyan Quadrilateral," in *WTTR,* 119-26. This article addresses some basic questions about the meaning of the Wesleyan quadrilateral, the relationships between Scripture, tradition, experience, and reason, and the justification and practicality of using these four sources and criteria for theological reflection. Abraham examines John Wesley's perspective on each of the four sources and criteria and then discusses the challenges for using them today.

ARM

Maddox, Randy, ed., *Aldersgate Reconsidered* (Nashville: Abingdon Press, 1990). This book is a series of articles about John Wesley's experience at Aldersgate from a variety of perspectives. At issue is the nature and interpretation of the impact of John Wesley's Aldersgate experience on the history of Methodism and its validity as a model of spirituality for Methodists today. The changing interpretations of the Aldersgate event reveal shifts in theological concerns in Wesleyan scholarship.

BOD

The Book of Discipline of The United Methodist Church (Nashville: United Methodist Publishing House, 1992). Published after each General Conference, *The Book of Discipline* is a guide for the church. It contains a summary of the history of The United Methodist Church, including the inheritance from the uniting Methodist and Evangelical United Brethren traditions, including the foundational documents, "The Articles of Religion," and the "Confession of Faith." The General Rules, doctrinal standards, and the theological task of The United Methodist Church are also included in the prefatory material. The remainder of the book deals with the organization of The United Methodist Church.

BOR
The Book of Resolutions of The United Methodist Church (Nashville: United Methodist Publishing House, 1992). Each General Conference approves resolutions to guide the church in consideration of current issues. With each edition of the *Book of Resolutions,* some resolutions are retained, new resolutions are added, and outdated resolutions are dropped. These resolutions become part of the policy of The United Methodist Church.

BOW
The Book of Worship of The United Methodist Church (Nashville: United Methodist Publishing House, 1992). The new *Book of Worship* provides guidance for conducting worship services in The United Methodist Church. It is a book of worship resources for seasons of the Christian year, special Sundays and other special days, and general acts of worship. The *Book of Worship* provides resources for a variety of settings and is purposely inclusive of ethnicity, culture, and gender.

Brueggemann, Walter. *Interpretation: Genesis* (Atlanta: John Knox Press, 1982). As a commentary for those who teach and preach the Bible, this book relies on the use of historical and theological work for understanding and interpreting the text. The goal is to invite the reader into dialogue with the author in order to discover the meaning of Scripture for life in today's world.

Carter, Warren. "Blessings on You," (chap. 3 in *The Sermon on the Mount: A Reader-Response Approach,* manuscript in process). This book begins by assuming that the Sermon on the Mount is an identity-forming, life-style-shaping document. In this chapter, the Beatitudes are examined as statements of vision and challenge. The discussion of the biblical text calls mainline Protestant churches to accountability for living as faithful people under God's rule.

COCU

The COCU Consensus: In Quest of a Church of Christ Uniting (Consultation on Church Union, 1985). This study book contains the statement recognized by the 1988 General Conference of The United Methodist Church and a study guide. Historical and current issues that divide the COCU churches are discussed and the objectives for the Consultation are examined. Statements regarding membership, confessing the faith, worship, and ministry are included in the consensus statement, which provides a working document for continuing dialogue.

Craddock, Fred B. *Interpretation: Luke* (Louisville, Ky.: John Knox Press, 1990). This commentary on Luke provides resources for persons who teach and preach. Particular attention is paid to Jesus' heritage in Judaism, as well as the development of the church following his death and resurrection. Scripture study culminates in interpretation of the gospel for Christians today.

Crosby, Michael H. *Spirituality of the Beatitudes: Matthew's Challenge for First World Christians* (New York: Orbis Books, 1982). Crosby focuses on the reign of God in this book, which emphasizes the relevance of the gospel for modern living. A chapter on each of the Beatitudes seeks to define God's reign and the life-style of those who seek to live under God's rule.

DSTT

Doctrinal Standards and Our Theological Task (Nashville: Graded Press, 1989). This study book is a very accessible reprint of Part 2 of the *Book of Discipline,* which includes the doctrinal heritage, the historical background, the doctrinal standards, and the theological task of The United Methodist Church.

DSTTLG

Carder, Kenneth L. *Doctrinal Standards and Our Theological Task: Leader's Guide* (Nashville: Graded Press, 1989). The leader's guide to Part 2 of the *Book of Discipline* outlines study session plans for reflecting on the doctrinal standards and the theological task of The United Methodist Church. Each session includes grounding in Scripture, an examination of the doctrinal standards, and suggestions for discussion and interpretation.

GMKL

Langford, Thomas. *God Made Known* (Nashville: Abingdon Press, 1992). In this study book, Langford addresses the nature of the theological task for United Methodists by examining the relationship between doctrine and theological reflection. Langford also discusses the use of the Wesleyan quadrilateral of Scripture, tradition, experience, and reason as the sources and criteria for theological reflection before summarizing the principal doctrines from a United Methodist perspective.

GOGK

Kinghorn, Kenneth Cain. *The Gospel of Grace: The Way of Salvation in the Wesleyan Tradition* (Nashville: Abingdon Press, 1992). Kinghorn examines the doctrine of grace as the central message of the Bible. Grace is viewed through the perspective of John Wesley's understanding of the way of salvation beginning with creation and ending with sanctification.

Guelich, Robert A. *The Sermon on the Mount: A Foundation for Understanding* (Waco, Tex.: Word, 1982). This commentary on Matthew 5–7 examines the setting of the Beatitudes within the framework of the Gospel of Matthew. The author leads the reader through a literary analysis of the text and then comments on the meaning of the text for a life of faith.

Huebner, Dwayne, "Religious Education: Practicing the Presence of God," *Religious Education* 82 (Fall 1987): 572. Huebner begins with the Christian tradition of constant awareness or reference to God throughout the day. He assumes that the purpose of religious education is to help persons think about how they live in this world in relationship to God and people.

JWED

Cushman, Robert E. *John Wesley's Experimental Divinity: Studies in Methodist Doctrinal Standards* (Nashville: Abingdon Press, 1989). Cushman examines the background and meaning of John Wesley's practical or experimental divinity, asking why this idea has disappeared from American Methodism. His goal is to recover experimental divinity, particularly as a means to understanding the implications of the doctrinal standards for The United Methodist Church.

Karris, Robert J. *Luke: Artist and Theologian* (New York: Paulist Press, 1985). Karris bases his commentary on Luke on the assumption that the themes of the Gospel reveal the author's theological position. Karris particularly emphasizes the theme of justice through examination of Jesus' association with outcasts, concluding that Jesus' identification with the poor and oppressed teaches us God's way of life through words and actions.

LLDG

Gunter, W. Stephen. *The Limits of Love Divine* (Nashville: Abingdon Press, 1989). This book addresses John Wesley's struggles in understanding the nature of "love divine." It contains a thorough analysis of eighteenth-century anti-Methodist literature, which forced Wesley to clarify and articulate his understanding of the limits of love divine. The notes and selected bibliography of this book provide a wealth of resources for further study.

McKim, Donald K. *Theological Turning Points: Major Issues in Christian Thought* (Atlanta: John Knox Press, 1988). McKim summarizes the historical debate on principal theological doctrines like the Trinitarian controversy and the christological controversy. By examining the theological turning points in history, he enables Christians to address such issues as: Who is God? Jesus Christ? What is authority? What are the theological turning points today?

MMH

Heitzenrater, Richard P. *Mirror and Memory: Reflections on Early Methodism* (Nashville: Abingdon Press, 1989). Heitzenrater takes a new look at the significance of early Methodist history in light of his discoveries of primary source material. The book not only provides a call to responsible scholarship in Methodist studies, but also challenges United Methodists to remember the vision of their heritage.

Moore, Mary Elizabeth. "The Style and Substance of United Methodist Theology in Transition," *Quarterly Review* 9 (Fall 1989): 44-63. Moore addresses the issue of how United Methodists do theology. She names marks of United Methodist theology and then discusses shifts in theological statements from the 1972–1988 General Conferences. Moore concludes her article by naming the challenges for future theological reflection in The United Methodist Church.

MWFC

Clarke, Adam. *Memoirs of the Wesley Family* (New York: Lane & Tippett, 1976). This book was written in 1822 in response to a request from the 1821 Methodist Conference. Clarke was charged with collecting and arranging Wesley materials, both documents and anecdotes from remaining contemporaries. This attempt at historical accuracy resulted in this publication of primary documents and firsthand accounts from John Wesley's life.

The New Oxford Annotated Bible with the Apocrypha: An Ecumenical Study Bible (Oxford: Oxford University, 1991). Biblical scholarship and the discovery of new documents has led to the updating of the Revised Standard Version of the Bible. This volume of the New Revised Standard Version contains extensive annotations with cross-references. Essays on the historical, religious, and literary aspects of the Bible have been rewritten or updated.

Palmer, Parker. "The Clearness Committee: A Way of Discernment," *Weavings* 3 (July/August 1988): 37-40. Palmer describes the Quaker practice of a clearness committee and offers it as a means for dealing with dilemmas in the church. The clearness committee can provide a channel for the working of the Holy Spirit in human decision making.

Phillips, J. B., *Your God Is Too Small* (New York: Macmillan, 1962). In this classic study book, Phillips addresses the limits that humans put around who God is and what God can do. Phillips describes a series of "unreal" gods and offers help in constructing an adequate view of God based on the recognition that Jesus Christ is where God is revealed most clearly. The book is dated and exclusive in language, but the images Phillips uses for limited understandings of God still resonate with readers.

Richey, Russell E. "The Role of History in the Discipline," *Quarterly Review* 9 (Winter 1989): 3-20. Why Methodists introduce themselves historically and define their doctrine historically in the *Book of Discipline* is Richey's primary question. He asserts that this practice is not only distinctive, but significant, and concludes that Methodist history is a statement of belief about God's action in the world.

Runyon, Theodore H. "The Importance of Experience for Faith," in *ARM,* 93-108. Runyon examines John Wesley's understanding of religious experience as the relationship and interaction between God and humans. God is the source of religious experience, and transformation is the result. Runyon evaluates John Wesley's Aldersgate experience in light of the meaning of religious experience and draws implications for Methodism in the twentieth century.

Stein, K. James. "Doctrine, Theology, and Life in the Foundational Documents of the United Methodist Church," *Quarterly Review* 8

(Fall 1988): 42-62. Stein compares the development of the Methodist and Evangelical United Brethren movements that led to the formulation of "The Articles of Religion" and the "Confession of Faith" as foundational documents for The United Methodist Church. Stein concludes this article with a discussion of the problems and possibilities of the foundational documents for the life of the church.

TWBM

Madsen, Norman P. *This We Believe* (Nashville: Graded Press, 1987). This study book offers historical background for "The Articles of Religion" of The Methodist Church and the "Confession of Faith" from The Evangelical United Brethren Church. Each session compares statements on similar theological themes from both of these foundational documents with biblical and historical foundations. Madsen then provides guidance for discussing the importance of the theological theme (belief) for The United Methodist Church.

UMH

The United Methodist Hymnal (Nashville: United Methodist Publishing House, 1989). The revised *United Methodist Hymnal* begins with John Wesley's directions for singing. Hymns are arranged in theological order beginning with the Trinity, followed by the church, and a vision of the reign of God. A variety of hymns and other worship resources that represent the diverse membership of The United Methodist Church are provided.

Walker, Williston. *A History of the Christian Church* (New York: Scribner's, 1985). This classic text on the history of the church from the first through the twentieth centuries has been revised in light of recent scholarship in this fourth edition. It provides insight into leading periods and movements in the history of the church.

Wimberly, Anne Streaty, and Edward Powell Wimberly. *Language of Hospitality: Intercultural Relations in the Household of God*

(Nashville: Cokesbury, 1991). Concern for language that would be appropriate to a racially inclusive church led to the development of this study document. It is a guidebook to help those who are part of God's household communicate in ways that witness to the partnership of all of God's people.

WJW

The Works of John Wesley, ed. Frank Baker, Richard Heitzenrater (Nashville: Abingdon Press, 1975–). This multi-volume series is an updated version of John Wesley's works based on scholarship from around the world. Newly discovered primary sources and exhaustive scholarship contribute to the extensive footnotes, which provide important information about historical background, implicit references, and central themes in Wesley's work.

WSMT

What Should Methodists Teach? Wesleyan Tradition and Modern Diversity, ed. M. Douglas Meeks (Nashville: Abingdon Press, 1990). This collection brings a variety of writers together to address issues of an increasingly diverse church in terms of its theological, social, and cultural make-up. In the final chapter, Meeks summarizes the issues raised in the book and names the tasks that still face the Methodist family.

WTH

Words That Hurt, Words That Heal: Language About God and People (Nashville: Graded Press, 1990). The 1984 General Conference of The United Methodist Church recommended a churchwide study on the issue of language. The recommendation was continued for 1988–92. This study considers issues of biblical and theological language about God and people and how to interpret our faith in inclusive ways. The study book includes a leader's guide and excerpts from interviews with eleven persons.

WTSL

Langford, Thomas A., ed. *Wesleyan Theology: A Sourcebook* (Durham, N.C.: Labyrinth Press, 1984). Langford has selected a series of writings and addresses from the Methodist tradition to illustrate the development of doctrine in the Wesleyan tradition. Langford provides short introductions to set the context for writings by persons like John Fletcher, Adam Clarke, Francis Asbury, Phoebe Palmer, Georgia Harkness, and Albert Outler.

WTTR

Runyon, Theodore, ed. *Wesleyan Theology Today: A Bicentennial Theological Consultation* (Nashville: United Methodist Publishing House, 1985). This work is the result of a consultation of two hundred persons who gathered in August 1983 to make a critical examination of various elements of the Wesleyan tradition. The articles represent issues discussed by eleven working groups, which focused on such topics as mission and evangelism, ecumenicism, spirituality and perfection, constructive theology, biblical authority, liberation theologies, and Christian social ethics.

3

Key Scripture References

1. PREPARATION FOR THE JOURNEY

Scripture Pairs for Comparison: Hos. 11:1 and Matt. 2:15; Ps. 22:1 and Matt. 27:46; Ps. 37:1 and Matt. 5:5; Isa. 63:16, 64:8 and Matt. 6:9; Hos. 6:6 and Matt. 9:13; Mal. 3:1 and Matt. 11:10; Jer. 32:17 and Matt. 19:26; Deut. 24:14-15 and Matt. 20:8; Ps. 41:9 and Matt. 26:24; Ezek. 23:31-34 and Matt. 26:39.

Journey: Gen. 33:12, 46:1; Exod. 3:18, 8:27; Deut. 1:7, 1:40, 2:1; 1 Sam. 15:18; Neh. 2:7; Matt. 10:10; Mark 6:8, 13:34; Luke 2:44, 9:3, 15:13; Rom. 15:24.

2. COME, O THOU TRAVELER UNKNOWN

A Tale of Deceipt and Blessing: Gen. 27:1-45, 28:10-22, 32:1–33:17.

Blessing: Gen. 22:17, 39:5; Exod. 32:29; Deut. 11:26-29, 12:15, 16:17; Pss. 3:8, 24:5, 109:17, 129:8, 133:3; Isa. 19:24, 44:3, 65:8; Rom. 15:29; 1 Cor. 10:16; 1 Pet. 3:9; Gal. 3:14.

Covenant: Gen. 21:17, 21:32, 26:28, 31:44; Exod. 2:24; Deut. 4:13, 23, 31, 5:2, 29:1, 9, 12, 13; Pss. 25:10, 14, 44:17, 50:5, 16, 55:20, 74:20, 78:10, 37, 89:3, 28, 34, 39, 103:18, 105:8, 9, 10; Isa. 59:21, 61:8; Luke 1:72; Acts 3:25; Gal. 3:17.

Salvation by Faith: Isa. 55:7; Eph. 2:8-10; Gen. 49:18; Pss. 3:8, 13:5,

14:7, 20:5, 24:5, 25:5, 27:1, 98:2; Isa. 12:2-3, 33:2, 49:6, 51:6; Luke 2:30; Acts 4:2, 13:26, 47, 16:17, 28:28; Rom. 1:16, 10:10, 11:11, 13:11; 2 Cor. 1:6, 2:2, 7:10; Phil. 1:19, 28, 2:12; 1 Pet. 1:5, 9, 10; Rev. 7:10, 12:10, 19:1.

God's Blessing, Our Invitation: Matt. 1:23, 4:17, 4:18-22, 5–7, 5:1-11, 12:28, 16:23, 18:20, 18:21-35, 28:20; Gen. 12:1-3; Pss. 24:1, 24:4, 37:11, 116:13; Isa. 55:1-2, 66:2.

God's Kingdom: Matt. 6:10, 33, 7:21, 9:35, 10:7, 12:28, 13:11, 24, 31, 33, 43, 45, 47, 52; Mark 1:14-15, 4:11, 9:1, 12:34, 14:25; Luke 1:33, 4:43, 8:1, 9:2, 60, 10:9, 11, 12:31, 17:20-21, 18:16-17, 22:16, 18; 23:42; John 18:36; Acts 8:12, 19:8, 20:25; 1 Cor. 4:20, 6:9-10; Eph. 5:5; Col. 1:30, 4:11.

3. 'TIS LOVE! 'TIS LOVE!

Father/Creator: Eccles. 12:1; Isa. 40:28, 43:15; Matt. 5:16, 45, 48; 6:1, 4, 6, 8, 9, 14, 18, 26, 32; Mark 14:36; Luke 10:21-22, 15:18; John 1:14, 3:35, 4:23; Rom. 1:25; 2 Cor. 1:2-3; 1 Pet. 4:19; 1 John 2.

Son/Lord: Matt. 8; Mark 11; Luke 13; John 11; Rom. 1:3, 7, 5:1, 11, 21; 1 Cor. 1:2, 3, 7-10; Philem. 3.

Spirit: Gen. 1:2; Judg. 3:10, 6:34, 9:23, 11:29, 13:25, 14:6, 19; Isa. 61:1; Ezek. 11:5, 24; Matt. 3:16; Mark 1:10; Luke 4:1, 14, 18, 11:13; John 1:32-33, 3:5-8, 14:17, 15:16, 16:13; 1 Cor. 12; Eph. 4:3-4.

Relationship Between Father/Son/Spirit: Deut. 6:4; Matt. 28:19; John 1:1-18, 1:32-34, 5:19-24, 5:31-38, 10:11-18, 12:44-50, 14:1-7, 14:25-31, 15:26-27, 16:13-15; Rom. 8:2; 1 Cor. 1:30, 13; 2 Cor. 5:18-19, 13:13, 14; Gal. 2:19*b*-20; Eph. 1:9-10, 4:4-6; Col. 1:15-20.

4. THROUGH FAITH I SEE THEE FACE TO FACE

God's Invitation: Luke 14:16-23; 1 Cor. 14:33; Heb. 5:9, 12:2.

Forgiveness: Exod. 32:32; Pss. 25:18, 86:5; Jer. 18:23, 31:34, 36:33; Matt. 9:2, 5; Mark 2:5, 9, 4:12; Luke 5:20, 23, 6:37, 7:47-48; Acts 5:31, 8:22, 13:38, 26:18; Rom. 4:7; Eph. 4:32; Col. 1:14, 2:13; James 5:15; 1 John 1:9, 2:12.

Creator/Created: Gen. 1–2; Eccles. 12:1; Isa. 40:28, 43:1, 7, 45:18; Jer. 31:22; Rom. 1:25; Eph. 2:10, 3:9, 4:24; Col. 1:16, 3:10; 1 Pet. 4:19.

Way of Salvation: Mark 14; Luke 22; John 12–13; 1 Cor. 5:7, 10:16-17, 11:20-22.

Redeemer/Redemption: Job 19:25; Pss. 19:14, 78:35; Isa. 41:14, 43:14, 44:6, 24, 47:4, 48:17, 49:7, 26, 54:5, 8, 59:20, 60:16, 63:16; Jer. 50:34; Acts 9:12, 15; Rom. 3:24, 8:23; 1 Cor. 1:30; Eph. 1:7, 14, 4:30; Col. 1:14.

Righteousness: Pss. 5:8, 17:15, 23:5, 71:2, 15, 16, 19, 24; Isa. 51:1, 5-8; Matt. 3:15, 5:6; Rom. 5:17-18, 21, 6:13, 16, 18-20; Phil. 1:11, 3:6-9.

Neighbor: Matt. 5:43-46, 19:19, 22, 37-39; Mark 12:31, 33; Luke 10; John 13:34-35, 14:15, 15:9-17; Rom. 13:9-10, 15:2; 1 Cor. 16:22-24; Gal. 5:6, 22; Eph. 2:4, 3:17, 4:25, 5:2; 1 Thess. 1:3, 3:12, 4:9; 2 Thess. 3:5; 1 John 4.

5. THE GOD WE WORSHIP

Naming God: Exod. 3:13-15.

Faith: Matt. 9:2, 22, 29; Luke 7:50; Rom. 1:5, 8, 12, 17, 4:5-20; 1 Cor. 12:9, 13:2, 13, 16:13; Gal. 2:16, 20, 5:5, 6, 22; Eph. 4:5, 13; 1 Thess. 1:3, 3:2, 5, 6, 7, 10; Heb. 11; James 2.

Hospitality/Brotherhood: Matt. 5:22-24; Rom. 12:13; 1 Tim. 3:2; Titus 1:8; Heb. 8:11; 1 John 2:9-11, 3:10-17, 4:20-21; 1 Pet. 2:17, 4:9.

4
Relevant United Methodist Documents and Hymns

1. PREPARATION FOR THE JOURNEY

Book of Discipline (BOD):

Pages 74-76	"The Nature of Our Theological Task"
Pages 76-82	"Theological Guidelines: Sources and Criteria"
Pages 82-85	"The Present Challenge to Theology in the Church"

United Methodist Hymnal (UMH):

386-87	Come, O Thou Traveler Unknown
60	I'll Praise My Maker While I've Breath
62	All Creatures of Our God and King
75	All People That on Earth Do Dwell
87	What Gift Can We Bring
100	God, Whose Love Is Reigning o'er Us
102	Now Thank We All Our God
115	How Like a Gentle Spirit
117	O God, Our Help in Ages Past
127	Guide Me, O Thou Great Jehovah
128	He Leadeth Me: O Blessed Thought
135	Canticle of Moses and Miriam
136	The Lord's My Shepherd, I'll Not Want
140	Great Is Thy Faithfulness
142	If Thou But Suffer God to Guide Thee
434	Cuando El Pobre

452	My Faith Looks Up to Thee
454	Open My Eyes, That I May See
463	Lord, Speak to Me
464	I Will Trust in the Lord
467	Trust and Obey
473	Lead Me, Lord
474	Precious Lord, Take My Hand
477	For Illumination
489	For God's Gifts
493	Three Things We Pray
495	The Sufficiency of God
631	O Food to Pilgrims Given

2. COME, O THOU TRAVELER UNKNOWN

Book of Discipline:

Pages 9-20 "Historical Statement"
Pages 71-73 "The Nature, Design, and General Rules of Our United Societies"
Pages 77-78 "Scripture"

United Methodist Hymnal:

Faith

129	Give to the Winds Thy Fears
332	Spirit of Faith, Come Down
385	Let Us Plead for Faith Alone
392	Prayer for a New Heart
452	My Faith Looks Up to Thee
455	Not So in Haste, My Heart
505	When Our Confidence Is Shaken
508	Faith, While Trees Are Still in Blossom

524	Beams of Heaven as I Go
529	How Firm a Foundation
534	Be Still, My Soul
595	Whether the Word Be Preached or Read
606	Come, Let Us Use the Grace Divine
607	A Covenant Prayer in the Wesleyan Tradition
650	Give Me the Faith Which Can Remove
707	Hymn of Promise

Salvation

57	O For a Thousand Tongues to Sing
59	Mil Voces Para Celebrar
163	Ask Ye What Great Thing I Know
182	Word of God, Come Down on Earth
224	Good Christian Friends, Rejoice
225	Canticle of Simeon
248	On This Day Earth Shall Ring
310	He Lives
378	Amazing Grace
887	Affirmation from Romans 8:35, 37-39
888	Affirmation from 1 Corinthians 15:1-6; Col. 1:15-20

God's Kingdom

275	The Kingdom of God
426	Behold a Broken World
435	O God of Every Nation
440	Let There Be Light
449	Our Earth We Now Lament to See
555	Forward Through the Ages
569	We've a Story to Tell to the Nations
721	Christ the King
726	O Holy City, Seen of John
730	O Day of God, Draw Nigh

734 Canticle of Hope

3. 'TIS LOVE! 'TIS LOVE!

Book of Discipline:

Pages 9-20 "Historical Statement"
Pages 40-73 "Doctrinal Standards"
Pages 79-80 "Tradition"
Pages 83-84 "Ecumenical Commitment"

Book of Resolutions:

Page 382 "Support the Consultation on Church Union Proposal"
Page 205 "COCU Consensus: In Quest of a Church of Christ Uniting"

Book of Worship:

178 "Amen, Praise the Father"
426 "Heritage Sunday"

United Methodist Hymnal:

61 Come, Thou Almighty King
64 Holy, Holy, Holy! Lord God Almighty
65 ¡Santo! ¡Santo! ¡Santo!
76 Trinity Sunday
79 Holy God, We Praise Thy Name
85 We Believe in One True God
88 Maker, in Whom We Live
108 God Hath Spoken by the Prophets
109 Creating God, Your Fingers Trace
119 O God in Heaven

125	Canticle of Covenant Faithfulness
267	O Love, How Deep
447	Our Parent, by Whose Name
604	Praise and Thanksgiving Be to God
686	O Gladsome Light
880	The Nicene Creed
881	The Apostles' Creed, Traditional Version
886	The World Methodist Social Affirmation

4. THROUGH FAITH I SEE THEE FACE TO FACE

Book of Discipline:

Pages 44-48	"Our Distinctive Heritage as United Methodists"
Page 61	"Article X.—Of Good Works"
Page 68	"Article X.—Good Works"
Pages 80-81	"Experience"
Pages 87-107	"Social Principles"

Book of Resolutions:

Pages 31-52	"Social Principles"
Page 115	"AIDS and the Healing Ministry of the Church"
Page 125	"Responsible Parenthood"
Page 209	"Comprehensive Approach to Native American Ministries"
Page 219	"Dependent Care"
Page 256	"Global Racism"
Page 317	"Ministry to Runaway Children"
Page 401	"Appalachian Challenge"
Page 446	"Self-Help Efforts of Poor People"
Page 452	"Special Needs of Farm Workers"
Page 584	"Infant Formula Abuse"

United Methodist Hymnal:

Invitation/Holy Communion

7	Prayer of Invitation
26	Prayer of Invitation
339	Come, Sinners, to the Gospel Feast
344	Tú Has Venido a la Orilla
347	Spirit Song
350	Come, All of You
623	Here, O My Lord, I See Thee

Way of Salvation

121	There's a Wideness in God's Mercy
355	Depth of Mercy
363	And Can It Be That I Should Gain
368	My Hope Is Built
369	Blessed Assurance
383	This Is a Day of New Beginnings
384	Love Divine, All Loves Excelling
393	Spirit of the Living God
396	O Jesus, I Have Promised
401	For Holiness of Heart
408	The Gift of Love
410	I Want a Principle Within
419	I Am Thine, O Lord

Social Holiness

426	Behold a Broken World
427	Where Cross the Crowded Ways of Life
432	Jesu, Jesu
436	The Voice of God Is Calling
438	Forth in Thy Name, O Lord

5. THE GOD WE WORSHIP

Book of Discipline:

Pages 82-86 "The Present Challenge to Theology in the Church"
Pages 87-107 "Social Principles"

Book of Resolutions:

Page 162 "Affirming a Diversity of Language Usage in the United States"
Page 178 "The United Methodist Church and America's Native People"
Page 196 "A Charter for Racial Justice Policies in an Interdependent Global Community"
Page 206 "Comity Agreements Affecting Development of Native American Ministries by The United Methodist Church"
Page 248 "Elimination of Racism in The United Methodist Church"
Page 256 "Global Racism"
Page 263 "Guidelines for Interreligious Relationships, 'Called to Be Neighbors and Witnesses'"
Page 285 "History of Blacks in The United Methodist Church"
Page 345 "Prejudice Against Muslims and Arabs in the U.S.A."
Page 360 "Racial Harassment"
Page 366 "Rights of Native People of the Americas"

Book of Worship:

R38-40, Appendix D "Language Guidelines" (1992 United Methodist Book of Worship, Daily Christian Advocate, Advance Edition, vol. 3).
Page 291 "Wesley's Covenant Service"

United Methodist Hymnal:

104 Praising God of Many Names

105	God of Many Names
107	La Palabra Del Señor Es Recta
110	A Mighty Fortress Is Our God
111	How Can We Name a Love
114	Many Gifts, One Spirit
116	The God of Abraham Praise
119	O God in Heaven
120	Your Love, O God
548	In Christ There Is No East or West
552	Here, O Lord, Your Servants Gather
555	Forward Through the Ages
556	Litany for Christian Unity
560	Help Us Accept Each Other
607	A Covenant Prayer in the Wesleyan Tradition

Notes

Chapter 1: Preparation for the Journey

1. The term *Hebrew Bible* for the Old Testament is gaining wider usage in recognition of the heritage Christians have received from the Jewish faith.
2. "Religious Education: Practicing the Presence of God," *Religious Education* 82 (Fall 1987): 572.
3. For further information about this process, see Parker Palmer, "The Clearness Committee: A Way of Discernment," *Weavings* 3 (July-August 1988): 37-40.
4. "The Style and Substance of Methodist Theology in Transition," *Quarterly Review* 9 (Fall 1989): 45.

Chapter 2: Come, O Thou Traveler Unknown

1. *Genesis* (Atlanta: John Knox Press, 1982), 227.
2. Ibid., 242.
3. Ibid., 267.
4. July 29, 1725, *WJW,* 25, p. 175.
5. August 18, 1725, *WJW,* 25, p. 179.
6. April 22, 1738, *WJW,* 18, pp. 233-34.
7. May 14, 1738, letter to William Law, *WJW,* 25, pp. 540-41.
8. May 24, 1738, *WJW,* 18, pp. 249-50.
9. *JWED,* 35.
10. *WJW,* 1, pp. 117-18.
11. Ibid., p. 120, lines 25-27.
12. Ibid., p. 122, line 29.

13. Ibid., p. 128, lines 8-9.
14. Ibid., p. 118, lines 17-21.
15. Ibid., p. 127, line 32.
16. Ibid., p. 118, line 24.
17. Sources for this summary of the meaning of the Beatitudes include: Warren Carter, "Blessings on You," chapter 3 in manuscript in process; Michael H. Crosby, *Spirituality of the Beatitudes* (New York: Orbis Books, 1982); and Robert A. Guelich, *The Sermon on the Mount: A Foundation for Understanding* (Waco, Tex.: Word Books, 1982).
18. Letters from Samuel Wesley dated January 26, 1725, September 7, 1725, and July 18, 1727, in *WJW*, 25, pp. 157-59, 182, 227.

Chapter 3: 'Tis Love! 'Tis Love!

1. Donald K. McKim, *Theological Turning Points* (Atlanta: John Knox Press, 1988), 6.
2. K. James Stein, "Doctrine, Theology, and Life in the Foundational Documents of the United Methodist Church," *Quarterly Review* 8 (Fall 1988): 43.
3. For further discussion of Irenaeus' position, see Williston Walker, *A History of the Christian Church* (New York: Scribner's, 1985), 77-79.
4. *Theological Turning Points*, 8.
5. Ibid., 43.
6. *TWBM*, 20.
7. "The Role of History in the Discipline," *Quarterly Review* 9 (Winter 1989): 8.
8. Stein, "Doctrine, Theology, and Life," 43.
9. Ibid.
10. Ibid., 57.
11. Ibid.
12. Ibid.
13. Ibid., 58-60.
14. *WTSL*, 19.
15. *COCU*, 55.
16. Ibid., 1.
17. Ibid.
18. Ibid., 2.
19. Ibid., 1.
20. Ibid., 2.
21. Ibid., 30.
22. Ibid., 31.
23. Ibid., 29.

Chapter 4: Through Faith I See Thee Face to Face

1. *Interpretation: Luke* (Louisville, Ky.: John Knox Press, 1990), 179.
2. Robert J. Karris, *Luke: Artist and Theologian* (New York: Paulist Press, 1985), 61.
3. Ibid.
4. *Interpretation: Luke,* 178.
5. *JWED,* 39.
6. William J. Abraham, "The Wesleyan Quadrilateral," in *WTTR,* 119-25.
7. *LLDG,* 276.
8. "The Importance of Experience for Faith," in *ARM,* 99.
9. *GOGK,* 68.
10. *LLDG,* 247.
11. Letter of October 19, 1725, *WJW,* 25, pp. 182-83.
12. *WJW,* 2, p. 535.
13. Ibid., p. 548.
14. Letter of November 10, 1725, from Susanna Wesley to John Wesley, *WJW,* 25, p. 185.
15. Letter of December 10, 1734, to Samuel Wesley, *WJW,* 25, p. 398.
16. Letter of January 13, 1710, *MWFC,* 347-48.
17. *WJW,* 1, #3, p. 426.
18. "Character of a Methodist," *WJW,* 9, #9, p. 37.
19. Letter of December 10, 1734, to Samuel Wesley, *WJW,* 25, p. 404.
20. *LLDG,* 265.
21. Ibid., 266.

Chapter 5: The God We Worship

1. *Your God Is Too Small* (New York: Macmillan, 1961), 7.
2. Words Copyright © 1975 by Hope Publishing Co., Carol Stream, IL 60188. All rights reserved. Used by permission.
3. Bruce M. Metzger for the committee, *The New Oxford Annotated Bible* (New York: Oxford University Press, 1991), xiv.
4. *Words That Hurt, Words That Heal: Language About God and People* (Nashville: Graded Press, 1990), 5.
5. Anne Streaty Wimberly and Edward Powell Wimberly, *Language of Hospitality: Intercultural Relations in the Household of God* (Nashville: Cokesbury, 1991), 23-24.
6. Ibid., 15.

Index